TORN ASUNDER

TORN ASUNDER

THE CIVIL WAR AND
THE 1906 DIVISION OF THE DISCIPLES

BEN BREWSTER

COLLEGE PRESS PUBLISHING COMPANY· JOPLIN, MISSOURI

Dedicated to ...

my mother, Lorna Brewster, who taught me to love history

and

my father, Andrew Brewster, who taught me to love my
Christian heritage

Endorsements for
Torn Asunder

"*B*en Brewster has examined the rich mother lode of primary documents to make a compelling case for the claim that the War Between the States, the American Christian Missionary Society, and/or instrumental music were NOT the driving forces behind the church split that was "officially recognized" in the 1906 census. The inherent human factors that surface in church conflicts provide Brewster with an abundance of examples of how leaders struggle for consistency in their philosophical positions, publications and preaching. Brewster capably develops his thesis that a uniquely American movement grounded in a quest for unity among the believers was ironically sabotaged by the irreconcilable differences among its leaders and their approach to biblical hermeneutics. This brief but fresh account of the American Restoration Movement, replete with its mystery, intrigue, and alliances of strange bedfellows reminds us that every solution to one problem in the church creates a fertile seedbed for an array of entirely new and potentially divisive problems for the next generation of leaders."

Bob Brewer, Ph.D.
Preaching Minister
Oxford Church of Christ
Oxford, Mississippi

"Pulitzer prize winning author, David C. McCullough, has said, "History is a guide to navigation in perilous times. History is who we are and why we are the way we are." If ever his words rang true, it is with regard to the changing times, conventions and beliefs of American religious history. It is especially descriptive of the church as it appears today in America.

Ben Brewster is a passionate student of restoration history who looks at it first with the eyes of factuality, then with the eyes of compassion, and finally with the eyes of conviction. He, like many of us who, though not always in agreement with the conclusions and positions espoused, cherishes our connection with this history and understands its value in searching out our own salvation. His deep and abiding admiration of those individuals who labored through the early days of reason and rediscovery in search of the true first century church is evident; however, it does not overshadow his integrity in presenting the past complete with its victories and flaws. He then is content to allow each of us to draw our own conclusions as to the value and validity of each principle, practice and position.

I'm not sure of their origins, but during my childhood, my father often shared two of his favorite maxims with me. First, "Learn from the mistakes of others. You don't have time to make them all yourself;" and, second, "If a road is cut through the woods, travel it as long as it is going in the right direction." This book helps us to look and learn from the past and at times may open a road in our minds going in the right direction.

I'm happy to recommend this book to you and to commend its author for taking the time to put it in our hands."

Dan Coffel
Minister
Eastwood Church of Christ
Haughton, Louisiana

"Torn Asunder is an excellent review of the controversies that faced the early leaders of the Restoration Movement and is relevant to us as even today we continue to strive for Christian unity. Jesus' words continue to challenge us: 'A new command I give you: love one another. As I have loved you, so you must love one another. By this all men will know that you are my disciples, if you love one another' (John 13:34-35)."

Larry Kirkeby, Elder
On behalf of the elders at the Airline Drive Church of Christ
Bossier City, Louisiana

Table of Contents

Acknowledgements

Writing a book is at once an extraordinary and an ordinary feat. It takes time, patience, and perseverance. Yet, the world is not experiencing any shortage of books.

In the writing of this book, I have learned the importance of being surrounded by a supportive team. Although my name is on the cover of this book, there are many others who sacrificed their time to see this book become a reality.

Special thanks are extended to Jerry Harris, Charles Beckham, Troy Freeman, Hop Paden, Larry Kirkeby, Curtis Marsh, and Buddy Stanley. These men serve as my elders at the Airline Drive Church of Christ. I appreciate their support and prayers during this project.

Jerry Harris did an amazing job designing the book cover, and I am honored by his talent and his desire to be a part of this book.

I am grateful for the input provided by Dr. James North, professor of church history at Cincinnati Bible Seminary, who first read the manuscript when it was completed in thesis form in 1999. Thank you for reminding me of the common heritage we share.

Thanks to Dr. Bob Brewer, Dan Coffel, and Hop Paden for reading this book in its "rough draft" form and providing much needed guidance.

Many thanks also go to those who assisted with research and editing. I owe a debt to Carol Coffel, the Airline Drive Church of Christ secretary, and to Carla Offutt, my assistant, who put in so much time editing and correcting my mistakes. Thanks also to Tom Edwards, for assisting me with some of the research.

Thanks also to Steve Jennings and College Press for the work they did behind the scenes and for the use of the pictures throughout the book.

My wife, Mendy, has also spent hours reading through the pages of this manuscript and making my sometimes confusing thoughts form gracefully into words.

And to my two children: Hannah and Drew. Thank you for inspiring me to dream. Continue this journey that your ancestors have walked for so many years, and, in the process, may you embrace the wonderful Christian heritage you have inherited.

Foreword

*A*s we enter the year 2006, we are experiencing the centennial of the official separation between the Christian Churches that worship with musical instruments and the Churches of Christ which do not. There are numerous efforts under way to mitigate this division, to soften the effects of what our forefathers did so many decades ago. Many of us find these efforts refreshing and hopeful, a reminder of the original goal of Christian unity that the founders of the Restoration Movement set a century before the unfortunate separation of 1906.

As a result, we welcome all efforts to understand the dynamics of the issues that led to that separation. Certainly one of the key players in that struggle was David Lipscomb, the highly respected editor of the *Gospel Advocate*, and long a spokesman for those who bristled at the use of musical instruments in worship as well as missionary organizations to carry on the churches' work of evangelism. In turn, Lipscomb was the product of various influences that led to his commitments—family background, personal relationships, and political ideology.

Ben Brewster's treatment of the issues that led to the division, and Lipscomb's role in them, is a helpful addition to this needed study. His work is solidly researched, fluently presented, and carefully argued. Anyone wanting to know more about the background of the division of 1906 can profit from reading this book. It will enlighten, challenge, and stimulate. The Restoration Movement needs more young men like Brewster with his firm commitments and gentle tolerance.

James B. North, Ph.D.
Professor of Church History
Cincinnati Christian University and Bible Seminary

Introduction

Iam a member of the Church of Christ. It is the church that is mentioned throughout the pages of the New Testament in the Bible. It is the church that Jesus founded.

I was added to God's church, just like those who professed their faith in Jesus and were baptized, were added in the first century.

As I read my Bible I find that Jesus established one church, made up of all those who put their faith in Jesus and obey his commands.

Yet, somewhere along the line the gift of unity among followers of Christ has degenerated into division. Christians have broken fellowship with one another. Heretics have been burned. Apostasy has been decried. Clashes over interpreting the sacred Scriptures have led to unholy wars among God's people, and we have lost our way.

I believe in the catholicity of the church. That is not to say that I am a Roman Catholic. I am a Christian who believes that the Bible reveals that there is one church, hence the term catholic, which simply means universal. However, something has happened since Christ established the church. The one church became many churches. Sects were formed which became denominations and we now live in a world with a religious landscape that is as numerous as it is confusing.

Growing up, I heard all kinds of theories as to why this is the case. Preachers and teachers postulated about why this is the situation. Of course, they were always pointing the finger at someone else. But there was one preacher who responded differently. There was one preacher who is as committed as any person I have ever met when it comes to following the Scriptures. That preacher is my father.

Since I was young, my father has taught me that the final authority for Christian faith and practice is the Bible. He has also taught me to be a bridge builder, to never compromise truth, but to reach out and initiate conversations with others.

In grade school, I became friends with a boy in my class whose dad was a preacher for what was called an independent Christian church. We played together, spent time at each other's homes, and at times, I would try to listen as our fathers talked with one another. Watching that interaction between our fathers impressed upon me that Christians, though disagreeing, can practice civility and attempt to find common ground.

Yet, in growing up in the Churches of Christ, I heard from others messages of exclusiveness, harsh rhetoric directed toward those with different names on their church buildings, and an unwillingness to have conversations or to simply be civil.

The explanations I heard from others never seemed to add up. So, to the delight of my mother, who is a high school history teacher, I began to peruse the pages of history, in particular, my religious heritage.

Every summer vacation my family took involved a stop at either a Civil War historical site or an American Restoration Movement historical site. If my parents were particularly adventurous, we would fit two stops into one trip.

At the time, I could not understand my father's excitement at standing inside the Cane Ridge Meeting House, or walking through Alexander Campbell's mansion. Why an old building called the Old Mulkey Meeting House mesmerized him, I did not understand. But now after exploring our heritage, I am beginning to understand.

I am proud of my heritage in the Churches of Christ. My family roots go back at least four generations in the American Restoration Movement. I have heard about our history from my father and from my grandfather, who loved Cane Ridge. His name was J.B. Adkins and he was a farmer in Kentucky. Many of the items found in the museum at Cane Ridge were donated by him. He had made the acquaintance of Franklin McGuire, a former curator at Cane Ridge, and the two made a bargain: "build a museum at Cane Ridge," my grandfather had offered, "and I will fill it."

Yet, my pride does not blind me to those particular pages in the history of the Churches of Christ that reveal dark moments, times when Christians cast aside the attitude of Christ in defending interpretations and also at times, defending truth.

My inability to reconcile our actions with the example of Christ led me on a quest. So far in the quest, I have discovered some of our best moments, times when we took the Great Commission to heart, initiated spiritual and faithful conversations, and truly exhibited the attitude of Christ in all our speech and activities. Despite the bleak moments in our history, there is no other place I would rather be. There is no other fellowship, no other faith, no other group of people that I would rather be a part of than the good people who comprise the Churches of Christ.

We have a wonderful heritage, and we must never forget our heritage. We walk in the steps of saints throughout history, from the first century to present. We continue together on this journey through life, seeking to follow God by searching the Scriptures, holding tightly to truth, and believing that better days are ahead.

So, why write this book? 2006 is an important year for Churches of Christ. It marks 100 years since Churches of Christ withdrew from what is called the American Restoration Movement. There were many issues involved and none more so than the question of biblical interpretation. This book tells the story of what happened, with a particular emphasis on the influence of the Civil War in the division.

This book is not a "tell-all." Many stories and historical anecdotes are left off the pages you will read. You will not find mention of "higher criticism" and the role this played in the division of the Movement. The focus of this book is on how the

Civil War affected adherents of the Movement. In this regard, I have attempted to deal with the primary issues that were swirling at the time and the leaders who found themselves often in disagreement with one another over these issues.

What you hold in your hands, was first written in 1999 as a thesis to fulfill the graduation requirements of a Master's Degree in Church History from the Cincinnati Bible Seminary. This seminary is associated with the Independent Christian Churches/Churches of Christ and it provided me with an experience I will always remember, none more memorable than one occasion in the class entitled "the Restoration Movement," taught by Dr. James B. North, who was also my advisor in graduate school.

As North expounded on the division within the Movement and the current state, namely the Churches of Christ, the Christian Churches, and the Disciples of Christ, he became very passionate toward those in the room who belittled "Church of Christ people" for being close-minded and intolerant. North forcefully dealt with this attitude as he proclaimed, while bringing his fists down on the podium, "They are our brothers in Christ!" The class sat silenced and stunned. And I sat with tears in my eyes and an aching heart realizing that for many in these two groups, sitting down together and talking is seen as impossible or unimportant.

I wish I could tell you that this book will lift your spirits. Unfortunately, this book is about division. Were there good reasons behind the division that was officially recognized in 1906? I'll let you be the judge. What I have attempted to do is compile a history of this particular period, in order to tell what happened and why.

Of course, some may see this work as biased and they are probably correct. I have spent my entire life in the Churches of Christ, so I am sure this experience has influenced what I have written. I hope that you, the reader, will come to admire the men whose stories fill this book. I hope that in seeing them in their best and worst moments that you will recognize them for who they were: humans. More importantly, they were Christian men seeking to follow God.

Note to the Reader: Throughout this book I have opted to use the term "Disciples" to describe members of the American Restoration Movement. This was the term that Alexander Campbell used and preferred. Of course others, like Rice Haggard and Barton Stone, preferred the designation "Christians," and you may as well. However, I have chosen the term "Disciples" to apply to all in the Movement at this time, and not to the Disciples of Christ, which, as a denomination, had yet to come into existence.

Ben Brewster
Bossier City, Louisiana
January 2006

"The Church of Christ upon earth is essentially, intentionally, and constitutionally one; consisting of all those in every place that profess their faith in Christ and obedience to him in all things according to the Scriptures, and that manifest the same by their tempers and conduct, and of none else; as none else can be truly and properly called Christians."

— *Thomas Campbell, 1809*

Birth of a Movement

*T*hroughout the history of Christianity, calls have sounded forth for reformation. Leaders have arisen who have called God's people back to God's ideal. Reformers have taken stands in order to ward off the threats to the purity of the Christian faith.

American history contains such a reformation. Commonly called the American Restoration Movement or the Stone-Campbell Movement, this reformation has left a permanent mark on America. This book is about this distinct Movement, beginning with a brief overview of its beginnings and ending with a sad commentary on what happened to divide a Movement committed to uniting all Christians.

The religious landscape in America in the 18th century was marked by the presence of state churches, which were supported by taxpayers. Such an arrangement presented the threat of the emergence of a national church, much in line with European practice. However, the competition between churches limited any one church's influence. The most important factor in the prevention of the establishment of a national church was the First Amendment, which took effect in 1791.

The 1787 Constitution had already guaranteed the voluntary church in America. Coupled with the First Amendment, this paved the way for religious pluralism. Such pluralism led to something called "sheep stealing." Churches were growing because of transfers and not by conversions. Interestingly, historians estimate that 90 percent of the American population was unchurched.

Abner Jones

The squabbling between churches was a turnoff to most Americans. People were not opposed to religion, but they were disgusted with the rancor between churches. This paved the way for what became known as "primitivism." This attitude emerged at the same time as individualism and both were directly influenced by the growth of the frontier. People on the frontier were individualists. They took care of themselves and did not seek help from centralized groups or government. They viewed government and bureaucracy as corrupt. During this time, public opinion rose as a primary religious authority. This was the state of America in which the country's largest indigenous religious movement was born.

In the latter part of the 1700s, men like Abner Jones and Elias Smith in the New England states began openly advocating a return to the primitive gospel. In fact, in 1801, Jones started a new church in Lyndon, Vermont, and called it simply a "Christian Church."

Elias Smith

Unknown to the Northern Christians, this call was also being heard in the Southern states. A powerful voice in the South for the cause of primitive Christianity belonged to James O'Kelly, a Methodist minister who left the Methodists in 1797. He was committed to two things: Christian union and the teaching of the Scriptures.

James O'Kelley

In 1808, the correspondence began to increase between the Northern and the Southern Christians. This led to an agreement on some foundational matters between the two groups. The groups agreed on three doctrinal positions: 1) Christ is the only head of the Church; 2) the New Testament is the only law for the Church; and 3) the name Christian is the only name for Christ's followers. This agreement was made in 1808.

Meanwhile, over in Kentucky (considered a part of the frontier at the time) the call to return to primitive Christianity was also ringing through the land. Barton Stone, who preached at the great Cane Ridge Revival in 1801, was championing a call to return to the basics of New Testament Christianity. Along with five other ministers, Stone left the Presbyterian church and formed a new group: the Springfield Presbytery. Seeing how the formation of such a group did more harm than good in terms of Christian unity, the men dissolved the group in 1804 in a document called *The Last Will and Testament of the Springfield Presbytery*. In this document were listed three basic ideas: 1) Christian unity, 2) exclusive biblical authority, and 3) local congregational autonomy.[1]

Barton Stone

Then in 1807, a man named Thomas Campbell arrived in Pennsylvania after leaving Northern Ireland and Scotland over his despair at the religious division and wrangling in his country. Shortly after arriving in Pennsylvania, Campbell began preaching under the oversight of a local presbytery in the western part of the state. In that same year, Campbell was charged with heresy and in 1808, he left the Presbyterians and began preaching in homes. In 1809, he continued to preach that reformation could only happen with a return to the Bible and he proclaimed, "Where the Scriptures speak, we speak; where the Scriptures are silent, we are silent."

Thomas Campbell

It was during this year, 1809, that Campbell wrote the most important document, next to the Bible, for what would become the American Restoration Movement: *The Declaration and Address*. He first read the document at a meeting on September 7, 1809. Two themes are present throughout the document: the unity of all Christians and a commitment to biblical authority, or as Campbell would put it, "union in truth."

In this document Campbell asserted that

The Church of Christ upon earth is essentially, intentionally, and constitutionally one; consisting of all those in every place that profess their faith in Christ and obedience to him in all things according to the Scriptures, and that manifest the same by their tempers and conduct, and of none else as none else can be truly and properly called Christians.[2]

He also claimed that "Nothing ought to be inculcated upon Christians as articles of faith; nor required of them as terms of communion, but what is expressly taught and enjoined upon them in the word of God." Here Campbell asserted that only what is expressly taught in the Bible is to be used as tests of faith and fellowship.

Alexander Campbell

Thomas' son, Alexander, arrived in America with the rest of the Campbell family this same year. The father-son tandem continued to challenge the religious establishment of the day and call people everywhere to simple, New Testament Christianity.

While the Campbells, along with Walter Scott, spread a message of reformation across Virginia (now West Virginia) and Ohio, Stone continued to call people to return to the Bible as their only sufficient guide for faith and practice.

The two movements continued to grow and in 1824, Alexander Campbell traveled to Georgetown, Kentucky, to meet Barton Stone. That meeting led to an extremely significant event in 1830 when a "Campbell" congregation and a "Stone" congregation merged in Millersburg, Kentucky. Yet, an even more significant event occurred on December 31, 1831 in Lexington, Kentucky, when representatives from the Campbell Movement and the Stone Movement met together. They discussed their similarities and their differences. In the end, union was consummated when Raccoon John Smith

John Smith

extended the right hand of fellowship to Barton Stone.

In 75 years, that union would come crashing down as the Movement officially splintered in 1906 when what became known as the "Churches of Christ" officially distanced themselves from the rest of the American Restoration Movement.

"It is again asked, why so zealous for Christian union? I answer, because I firmly believe that Jesus fervently prayed to his Father that believers might all be one – that the world might believe in him as sent by the Father."

— *Barton Stone, 1826*

The State of the Movement:

Pre-Civil War Developments

*T*he year was 1849. Zachary Taylor, a military hero, was President of the United States, thanks to a division within the ranks of the Whig Party. The Mexican War ended the previous year with the signing of the Treaty of Guadalupe Hidalgo, through which Texas officially became a part of the United States. And within a new religious movement, whose adherents simply called themselves Disciples, the seeds of division were beginning to sprout.

Tolbert Fanning, an influential leader in Tennessee, sounded the alarm in 1845 by claiming that the purity of the Movement was now besieged by apostasy. He wrote in the pages of the *Christian Review,*

No other proof is necessary to establish the fact, that an apostacy (sic) has commenced. The preachers and churches in many places, have evidently stopped at first principles, and have, from ignorance of the spiritual organization, practices and enjoyments of God's empire, and from an ambition to have a name amongst men, grown weary, and desire peace with the conflicting parties.[1]

Tolbert Fanning

Fanning was not the only leader to voice his reservations about the state of the Movement. Benjamin Franklin, an editor of a religious journal from Indiana, expressed negative feelings as well. Franklin believed that the

29

Benjamin Franklin

Movement was caught in a status-quo state, primarily because of poor preaching. The answer, according to Franklin, was a renewed emphasis on individual Bible study and prayer.

The formation of the American Christian Missionary Society in 1849 provided the fuel for an impending division within the ranks of the Disciples. The threat of division for a Movement based on unity and the authority of the Bible, was growing at an alarming rate. The cooperative missionary effort known as the ACMS was intended to pool the resources of this Movement for efficiency and success; however, some prominent individuals within what is commonly called the Restoration Movement opposed the ACMS. They saw the society as an innovation, and thus a departure from Thomas Campbell's famous pronouncement: "Where the Scriptures speak, we speak; where the Scriptures are silent, we are silent." They also held unswervingly to Campbell's premise stated in his famous *Declaration and Address* that anything without an expressive "Thus saith the Lord" would cause division and should be avoided.

The argument that silence of the Scriptures implies prohibition was not the only argument given in opposition to the ACMS. It was also argued that the only God-ordained missionary society was the local church. In accordance with this argument developed another view that if the church was the only God-ordained missionary society, then all other societies were not ordained by God and therefore were heretical.

Without a doubt, the raging debate on both sides of the society question caused havoc within the Movement and alienated friends. Ultimately, the missionary society served as a key issue in the division of the Disciples. The keys to this impending division were the similar methodologies used in the slavery and pacifism arguments, as well as the similar methodologies used in the missionary society and instrumental music arguments. The arguments used against the society were first used against slavery and for pacifism. What aided in bringing these arguments to a head was the increased organization of the

Disciples, seen most clearly in the development of the ACMS, which would drastically inflame the debates over the pressing social issues of the day.

What the Disciples now wrestled with were the pains that accompany growth in addition to a transition in leadership. These two matters provide the backdrop for what will happen during the Civil War.

This book focuses on the developing problems among the Disciples, the relation of the Civil War to the development of these ultimately divisive issues, and the impact of Southern leader and eventual editor of the *Gospel Advocate*, David Lipscomb. Despite being a relatively young, and somewhat unknown preacher among the Disciples in the years preceding the Civil War, several situations will take place during the War that will

David Lipscomb

forever color Lipscomb's views of the American Restoration Movement and propel him as one of the second-generation leaders.

Lipscomb's mentor was the previously mentioned, Fanning. In fact, Lipscomb adopted virtually every stance that Fanning took on major issues affecting the Disciples. Lipscomb saw Fanning's involvement in cooperative missionary efforts in Tennessee and also saw his mentor's fierce opposition to the continuance of a national missionary society for the Disciples.

Lipscomb was also indirectly influenced by Alexander Campbell. Lipscomb learned of Campbell through Fanning, who greatly admired the Disciple leader. Out of this admiration for Campbell, came a determination on the part of Lipscomb to remain true to the ideals of the Movement. To be true, in the mind of Lipscomb, was to firmly hold on to the simple and primitive religion espoused by the Movement's early pioneers. The only way Lipscomb knew how to do this was to stay status quo, and oppose any innovation.

The complex attitude of Lipscomb can be better understood by the effect that two pre-Civil War situations had upon him. The first involved Fanning and a professor from Bethany

Robert Richardson

College named Robert Richardson. The second involved a young, inspiring minister named Jesse Ferguson. This latter situation would affect Lipscomb the deepest.

In March, 1857, Richardson began a series of articles in the *Millennial Harbinger* (the most well-known publication among the Disciples) entitled, "Faith versus Philosophy." The matter which Fanning soon disputed with Richardson was the role of the Holy Spirit in conversion, which focuses in particular on how knowledge of God is derived. Richardson believed that such knowledge can derive from many sources, whereas Fanning adamantly maintained that the Bible alone was sufficient for such a task. This argument led Richardson to assume that Fanning believed "that man is incapable of learning the being and attributes of God from the works of nature." Richardson saw the works of nature as working in accord with divine methods to fully reveal the nature of God: "Natural theology proposes to prove the being and attributes of God from the works of nature, in harmony with Paul's declaration . . . 'For the invisible things of him from the creation of the world are clearly seen.'"[2]

Richardson argued that Fanning was merely taking the position of John Locke in that man is "wholly dependent upon revelation for all his ideas of God and spiritual things." In this regard, Richardson saw Fanning as a "victim" of philosophy.

Campbell took no part in the debate except to end it. The significance of this debate is that it simply mirrored the larger, growing conflict among the Disciples.

This question involving biblical interpretation haunted the leaders of the Movement and the problem of how to reconcile the views of Fanning and Richardson underwent a transformation between 1857 and 1865. Other issues continued to surface, but the underlying theme always revolved around the question of biblical interpretation. It was this thrust that was inflamed by the Civil War.

While the debate between Fanning and Richardson indirectly influenced Lipscomb, the situation with Ferguson deeply and directly affected him. The Ferguson situation proved to be a defining moment in the history of the Nashville Disciple churches.

The ideals of the American Restoration Movement had entered Tennessee as early as 1809 when John Mulkey and a large segment of the congregation where he preached made the commitment to follow no creed but the Bible. A congregation in Wilson County followed suit in 1816. In 1827, a congregation in Nashville separated from the Baptists over the Movement's call to primitive Christianity. Fanning had argued against the Nashville church hiring a "located" preacher. But in 1846, the congregation hired a 27-year old preacher named Jesse Ferguson. The relationship between Ferguson and the church appeared to blossom until trouble entered in 1852.

Jesse Ferguson

Few preachers among the Disciples ever rose to popularity as quickly as Ferguson. Before the age of 30 he served as the preacher for the largest Disciples' church in Nashville and was also serving as the editor for the *Christian Magazine*, begun by Fanning in 1844 (originally called the *Christian Review*). Ferguson was an effective preacher, debater, and writer. His reputation was so impressive among the Disciples that it was a surprise when he was branded as the Movement's first heretic.

The great controversy surrounding Ferguson dealt with his teachings on I Peter 3:18-20. Ferguson believed this text teaches that the dead have a second chance to respond to the gospel message. He based this belief upon the mention of Christ preaching to the spirits in prison. It was hardly a surprise that Disciples leaders, including Fanning, disputed such teaching. What was a surprise was that what Ferguson saw as a matter of opinion, other leaders saw as a matter of faith. One of those leaders was Campbell who took a firm stand against Ferguson and what he termed a "posthumous gospel." He did this primarily through the pages of the *Millennial Harbinger*, but he also made a trip to Nashville to confront this teaching. However, by this time, Ferguson was not to be persuaded.

Since the initial columns written by Campbell, the Nashville preacher had written that he communicated with the dead and he also did not believe in a literal hell. Ferguson refused to attend Campbell's meetings in Nashville because a spirit had warned him against doing such a thing.

Campbell believed that the I Peter text referred to those who lived during the time of Noah, who had the opportunity to repent before the flood. To Campbell, Ferguson's teaching was nothing less than heresy. He did not understand it practically and he most certainly did not understand it philosophically. The influence of Campbell, and his subsequent visit to Nashville, led the elders of Ferguson's congregation to ask him to resign.

The Ferguson situation shook the Disciples in Nashville. Ferguson was well-respected and extremely popular. His fall from grace was hard for some to handle, especially Lipscomb. As a student at Franklin College, the young Lipscomb took opportunity to listen to the preaching of Ferguson. He was fascinated by this enigmatic preacher. Lipscomb's respect and admiration for Ferguson made the situation that much harder for Lipscomb to deal with. Later in life, he shared these views, including his consideration of leaving the Movement. He wrote, "And as we were young, it seemed to us there must be something radically wrong in the organization and work of the church that could not prevent such disorders and disasters, so we looked around us to see if we could reconcile our convictions of right to some of the denominational positions."[3]

Others, like Fanning, felt betrayed. Fanning had brought Ferguson aboard as an editor for the *Christian Review*. Even though he opposed the church in Nashville hiring Ferguson (because of his opposition to located preachers), Fanning still supported and promoted Ferguson.

Then there were some like Campbell, who saw Ferguson's beliefs as not merely matters of opinion, but as heretical teachings that could do severe damage to the Movement if not confronted and silenced. More than anything, however, the Disciples, led by Campbell, drew a line of fellowship for the first time. What Campbell had done was state that there is a limit to free discussion. So Campbell, as the most influential leader in the Movement, felt he had no choice but to publicly oppose Ferguson, not as a brother, but as a heretic.

How this situation affected Lipscomb is a key to understanding the attitude and actions of the Nashville editor in the years preceding the official pronouncement of division. Lipscomb was a young, influential college student at the time of the Ferguson affair. He was also a great admirer of Ferguson. The situation that followed convinced Lipscomb that specific lines must be drawn to prevent future such occurrences. Lipscomb saw innovations such as the American Christian Missionary Society and the use of instrumental music in worship as departures from the teaching of the New Testament and the commitment of the Movement's pioneers to biblical authority. He could not reconcile the notion of unity without first establishing a foundation based solely upon the Scriptures. For that reason, Lipscomb held to a conservative view of the Bible, which equated silence with prohibition. If the Bible did not specifically authorize a practice, than that practice should be prohibited. Lipscomb's behavior was much like Campbell's in dealing with Ferguson. He believed that on some matters, opinions should not be publicly expressed. Lipscomb believed this true of anything not expressly taught in the Bible.

Despite the early problems within the Movement, the Disciples continued to grow, although slowly. The rise of frontierism and the attractive notion of a restoration of New Testament Christianity quickly enamored many who heard the pleas of these preachers who followed no creed but the Bible. The growth, though, brought problems. The larger an organization becomes, the harder it is to control individual members. New thoughts were developing, as well as strong opinions as to the direction that the Movement should take. What also developed was a desire to somehow bring together the many scattered congregations of Disciples in various states and join in a cooperative effort to evangelize the world.

The difficult question of cooperation was further clouded by a transition in leadership within the Movement. Barton W. Stone, who preached at the great Cane Ridge Revival in

Kentucky in 1801, and who is also considered one of the Movement's pioneers, died in 1844. His death is a significant fact in that despite the unity embraced between Stone and Campbell, there were distinct differences between the two regarding scriptural and non-scriptural matters. Yet, the unity was not achieved, but preserved. No one was more responsible for this than Stone. His efforts to unite the Christians with Campbell's Disciples (which took place in 1831), contributed a great deal to the ability of the Movement to not only survive, but begin a pattern of growth. Stone had long desired a united Christendom. In 1826, in the pages of his own journal, the *Christian Messenger*, he wrote, "It is again asked, why so zealous for Christian union? I answer, because I firmly believe that Jesus fervently prayed to his Father that believers might all be one—that the world might believe in him as sent by the Father."[4]

Stone had contributed much to the Movement. He had persevered even when others had abandoned the ideals of New Testament Christianity. He had protected the young churches in the Movement in Kentucky from the heresy of the Shakers, and he had filled an important role as an unshakable leader for a struggling Movement.

The men who followed Stone did not hold fast to that deep commitment to maintain unity. Even Campbell, who placed matters of faith above unity, would not find the loving nature of Stone among the next generation of leaders. However, he would possess a nearly equal commitment to unity as Stone did. In 1825, Campbell asserted that unity could only take place when the man-made foundations of religion gave way to the foundation of Christ. He candidly wrote, "When we have found ourselves out of the way we may seek for the ancient paths, but we are not at liberty to invent paths for our feet. We should return to the Lord."[5]

Though Stone was the first of the original pioneers to die, in the next few years several other preachers also died, thus leaving Campbell to work with a younger generation of leaders whose ideals proved to be somewhat of a different nature. In 1854, Campbell's father, Thomas, died. He was the great architect behind the 1809 *Declaration and Address*. This document has proven to be the single most important document, next to the Bible, for adherents of the American Restoration Movement. In it, the elder Campbell laid down some propositions that set the course for future generations.

The elder Campbell was followed in death by the successful evangelist of the Mahoning Baptist Association, Walter Scott, in 1861. Scott's passion was in sharing what he termed the "golden oracle," namely, that Jesus is the Son of God! He had developed a plan of evangelism that some churches still follow today. Scott's plan was simple: believe that Jesus is the Messiah, submit to baptism, and then God will forgive your sins and give you the Holy Spirit. His plan was hugely successful across the

Walter Scott

Western Reserve and Scott became known as the "evangelist" of the Movement. However, the beginning of the Civil War weighed heavily on Scott and he died shortly after the fall of Fort Sumter. It is ironic that one of the first generation leaders died the same year as the beginning of the Civil War.

What began as a noble cause, restoring New Testament Christianity, soon erupted into division as bitter rhetoric was exchanged between those in support of and those in opposition to such cooperative efforts. In addition to the missionary society, another issue surfaced: the use of instruments in worship. In 1859, L.L. Pinkerton, the minister for the church in Midway, Kentucky, brought a melodeon into the worship assembly. The effects of such an action were not seen, though, until after the Civil War. But it is safe to say that this was second only to the missionary society as the most destructive argument with which the Disciples grappled.

When the Civil War began, divisive discord was slowly building within the Movement. With the growing discord, however, was a growth in numbers. According to some estimates, the Disciples had grown to almost 200,000 adherents by 1860. Such growth was staggering, especially in view of the slow population growth nationally.

Nevertheless, the threat of division finally became a reality with the advent of the Civil War. Issues pushed ideologies to the forefront, which, in turn placed an emphasis on differences, instead of similarities. This was not the legacy left by Stone and Campbell, but it was the legacy Lipscomb inherited.

"We are not allowed to make our own private judgment, interpretation, or opinion, a ground of admission into, or of exclusion from, the Christian Church."

— *Alexander Campbell, 1845*

Slavery:

Matter of Faith or Opinion?

Slavery was among the most bitter of the issues underlying the Civil War. The arguments concerning slavery were moral arguments. Questions of the morality of owning slaves caused division throughout the United States. Despite the efforts of some Disciple leaders to keep this issue from dividing the Movement, it was implausible to restrain the opinions of the people who comprised the Movement.

The Disciples were not immune from the deeply divided opinions about slavery which surrounded the country. This debate infiltrated the ranks of the Disciples and caused brethren to choose sides on this matter. A difference of opinion was found even among the Movement's founding fathers concerning this explosive issue. Barton Stone condemned slavery and saw no justification for the continued practice of it. Alexander Campbell, on the other hand, would not condemn slavery and urged that the Disciples not make the issue a test of fellowship. Despite differing over the issue of slavery, Stone and Campbell still remained fiercely united. The next generation of leaders would never possess the unifying spirit of Stone and Campbell. Slavery was the first issue to exploit this disheartening fact.

The discussions concerning slavery were not limited to simply asking if whether such an institution was moral or not. Other questions took hold of the Disciples. There were those in the Movement who advocated abolitionism. There were others who genuinely believed in the superior status of the white race. Still others, while ardently opposing abolitionism, sought ways to rid the country of an institution that was not only dividing sections of the country, but (until the invention of the cotton gin) was also increasingly proving to be less economically feasible. If the only question was to the morality of slavery, then the issue would not have taken center stage in the Civil War and certainly would not have turned Disciples against one another. Yet, Disciples could not discuss the morality of slavery without invoking the use of the Bible, which in their minds was the sole basis for morality. With slavery and its many arguments, the Disciples found themselves watering their own seeds of division.

The study of Disciple opinions about slavery is important because it is one of the few major issues on which each leader in the first generation of the American Restoration Movement and the principal movers in the second generation expressed their views. For example, Thomas Campbell, Walter Scott, and Stone were silent on the instrumental music question. And while not totally silent on the missionary society issue, the recorded views of these three were extremely limited. Yet, with slavery, not only can one find what Stone, Scott and the Campbells thought, he can also find what Tolbert Fanning, David Lipscomb and Isaac Errett believed.

Despite the unity that Stone and Alexander Campbell shared in the midst of their differences, an examination of those who followed each man's respective views reveals the emergence of two distinct attitudes within the Movement. Stone and the Kentucky Christians held strong views when it came to issues of social justice, of which slavery was one. Because they tied together Christian faith with one's position on social issues, any differing opinion became a test of fellowship. This meant a limitation of fellowship with those either not subscribing to a particular view or those with other beliefs on the subject. Such is the case when one passionately believes in something. Most likely, that belief will become as important for the religious person as the very words of

Scripture. Those holding to the views of Stone melded opinions about slavery into the core of their religious beliefs.[1]

The test of fellowship was not something that Stone advocated and it was certainly something that Campbell desperately wanted to avoid. Campbell wrote at length in the *Millennial Harbinger* about the issue of slavery. He believed the matter belonged in the political arena and if allowed to rear its head among the Disciples, it would put a tremendous strain on fellowship, especially fellowship of the Disciples in different sections of the country.

Campbell had begun addressing the problem of slavery in his previous journal, the *Christian Baptist* as early as 1823. He saw the cruelty that the system promulgated, such as the reckless dividing of slave families. Campbell's protest of injustice, which he saw in the institution of slavery even led him into the political arena. He, like Stone, found the idea of colonization, whereby the slaves are freed and sent back to Africa, as the most attractive means for ending the problem. In 1832, he proposed legislation at the gathering of the Virginia House of Delegates which failed. At the time, Campbell had an unusual, and what some termed "radical" plan. Campbell advocated using the surplus from the United States treasury to free the slaves, compensate the owners, and then send the freed slaves back to their homeland "until the soil of our free and happy country shall not be trod by the foot of a slave, nor enriched by a drop of his sweat or blood, that all the world may believe that we are not a nation of hypocrites."[2]

The hypocrisy, as seen by Campbell, was evidenced by the national outcry against abuses in other countries, while a horrible abuse at home was perpetuated. Campbell wrote that the country did not hesitate to decry abuses in other countries "while we have millions of miserable human beings at home, held in involuntary bondage, in ignorance, degradation and vice, by a republican system of free slave-holding.[3] Disenchanted with the political world, Campbell returned to Bethany and continued his efforts at spreading the message about the restoration of New Testament Christianity.

Robert Richardson, the personal physician and close friend

to Campbell who wrote an extensive biography of the leader's life, disclosed Campbell's negative views of slavery. In spite of those views, Campbell still opposed those who attempted to use the Bible to prove the sinfulness of slavery. Richardson wrote that Campbell "felt it his duty" to oppose the extremists" and their attempts "to deny the lawfulness of the relation of master and servant, and to pervert the Scriptures." He felt it his duty to oppose their errors.[4]

By doing this, Campbell set himself up not only to be misinterpreted, but to also be severely criticized by the anti-slavery Disciples. Simply put, Campbell thought that what a person believes about slavery is not essential to Christian fellowship or salvation.

Stone was not as diplomatic as Campbell in his rhetoric about the slavery issue. By 1828, the issue was clear-cut for Stone. He pointedly wrote, "No man of intelligence now presumes to justify it, whether he be a politician, moralist, or Christian. He would blush in the attempt.[5]

The difference between Stone and Campbell is obvious. One viewed slavery as wrong, but still as a matter of opinion and not faith. The other viewed slavery as an evil that could not coexist with the Christian rule of faith.

The second generation of Disciple leaders mirrored the arguments of the first generation and continued to seriously debate the arguments as well. For the most part, the leaders recognized the political nature of the problem, and, because of this, were able to disagree without dividing. However, they could not stop slavery from planting seeds of division, some of which would not be noticed until forty years later.

Among the Southern Disciples who opposed slavery were Tolbert Fanning and David Lipscomb. Fanning had accompanied Campbell on a preaching tour in 1835 and 1836. Through this experience, he developed a deep respect for Campbell and his continual efforts at restoring simple, primitive Christianity. Yet, Fanning was not as restrained in his public comments about slavery as Campbell was. His motivation, though, for opposing slavery was similar to Campbell's. Fanning was deeply affected by witnessing firsthand the splitting of a slave family, in particular the removal of the father from his family so that he could be sold for profit.[6]

Fanning was not merely satisfied with keeping silent about the situation. In fact, he was once arrested after rebuking a slave owner during a sermon.[7] The fact that Fanning was arrested for such an action illustrates the strong feelings of Southerners about slavery.

In this issue and many others, Fanning had a tremendous influence on a young Tennessean named David Lipscomb. Not only was Fanning his mentor, but the two men developed a deep friendship.

Lipscomb was born January 21, 1831, in Tennessee. Later in his life, the deep love he had for Tennessee, the empathy he exhibited toward his fellow Tennesseans, and the passion he had for the development of the Disciples in his beloved state, became obvious.

Named after his grandfather, Lipscomb seemed destined to fill a place among the emerging Disciples in Tennessee. His grandfather had left the Baptists because of Campbell's writings in the *Christian Baptist*. His parents were also greatly influenced by Campbell's first journal. The family's decision to leave the Baptists was greatly influenced when the church of which they were a part, Beans Creek Baptist Church, rescinded their membership. Such was the religious transformation that Lipscomb witnessed as a young boy.[8]

Slavery was also a much discussed topic among the Lipscomb family. The family decided to free their slaves after becoming convinced the practice of slavery was inconsistent with the teachings of the New Testament. The problem, though, came when the state of Tennessee imposed the Exclusion Law of 1831, which stipulated that bond be paid for every freed slave and that every freed slave must leave the state. This was the primary reason the Lipscombs moved to Illinois for a brief period of time.[9]

However, the laws in Illinois concerning freed slaves were still developing, and the overall attitude was one that said freed slaves were unwelcome. The developing laws would concur with this attitude.

The Lipscomb family's venture west proved costly when Ann Lipscomb, David's mother, contracted malaria and died, along with three of David's siblings. The terrible cost suffered by the Lipscombs is indicative of their commitment to a cause. They believed that their slaves should be granted freedom. Their faithfulness to that belief led to great pain. One thing is certain: when the Lipscomb family developed a belief, they practiced it regardless of the cost. Certainly, this attitude is clearly seen in the later life of Lipscomb. However, the slavery issue was unavoidable for the Lipscombs when they returned to Tennessee. Virtually forced, by the state's strict laws to own slaves, the Lipscombs focused on treating their slaves with the utmost respect and dignity.

When Lipscomb reached the age of fifteen, his father sent him and his brother, William, to Franklin College. It was at Franklin College that Lipscomb met Fanning. The choice to send Lipscomb and his brother to this institution was precisely because it was Fanning's school. His reputation was well-known throughout Tennessee and "his converts to primitive Christianity were numerous; his fame widespread."[10]

Lipscomb's college years were spent during a time of emerging crisis over the slavery issue. The rising tide of dissension over this issue continued to gain momentum across the country. Those of religious faith were not exempt. Among the Disciples, there were men who vehemently condemned slavery and there were also men who believed that the institution was God-ordained. The emotion of the slavery argument rose to new levels with the invention of the cotton gin. The effect the cotton gin had on the Southern economy was tremendous. This invention brought an economical slant to the issue, and explained why Southerners fought against efforts at slave emancipation.[11]

There were also men who held private opinions and kept those opinions private. Lipscomb was one of these men. In Lipscomb's developing religious views, the discussion of slavery was nowhere near the core of following Jesus. This was the view also held by Campbell. Because of Lipscomb's developing views concerning the Christian's relation to government, especially his thought that the government was a man-made institution incapable of solving the major problems of the world, Lipscomb viewed the debate over slavery in a different light. Lipscomb's view of government put his beliefs about slavery in the camp of Stone. Yet, Lipscomb would also later become extremely active in social issues, particularly during the reconstruction period in the South. In fact, the social efforts of Lipscomb were extraordinary among the Disciples. Many in the Movement neglected the social needs of the day, many of which the church could address. Lipscomb saw the needs and addressed them.

In 1859, an Indiana Disciple named Benjamin Franklin, demonstrated the same thinking about the relation of slavery to the church that Campbell had espoused, and which a young Lipscomb was beginning to formulate. Franklin wrote an article in the *American Christian Review* entitled, "Our Position Called For." In this article he outlined the requirements to be met before the Disciples could engage in the discussion over the morality of slavery. His primary argument was that no position can be made unless Christ has expressly stated a position. He asked the probing question in the article, "Did the Lord and the Apostles do right in never deciding the question, whether slavery is right or wrong, discussing, and never saying one word about the question in any form?"[12]

The choice of argument for Franklin, silence of the Scriptures, is the same argument that he later used in opposing the missionary society and instrumental music in worship. It is within the framework of the debate over slavery that the ground was laid for further, more significant debates among the Disciples.

Despite the host of arguments concerning slavery, no one addressed the subject in more complete fashion than Campbell. Writing a series of articles in 1845 in the *Millennial Harbinger*, Campbell argued that slavery is a matter of opinion. He addressed the difference in holding views as a Christian and holding views as an American, and he pled for unity despite the already occurring division in the country. His argument for opinion is summed up in this statement: "We are not allowed to make our own private judgment, interpretation, or opinion, a ground of admission into, or of exclusion from, the Christian church."[13]

While Campbell's words were received favorably by a majority of the Disciples, others turned a deaf ear to his advice. The reason was the Civil War. No event in the history of the United States polarized the country as much as the Civil War. Sectional battle lines were drawn and a young nation found itself thrust into the throes of a most horrible controversy.

In the midst of the sweeping call to arms and passionate calls from the Union and Confederacy, the Disciples struggled for loyalty as to the very reason for existence: unity based upon the Bible. Unfortunately, the Disciples lost sight of this and had their vision clouded by the seduction of sectionalism. The effects of the slavery debate on the Disciples did not become fully apparent until after the Civil War, when it became painfully obvious that a division had taken place in their ranks.

For a native Southerner like Lipscomb, it was impossible to escape the influence of sectionalism. The reason was not the slavery issue; that was but a minor detail for Lipscomb. He believed that the only healing the country could have was in a united group of believers proclaiming the message of Jesus Christ. This was the belief that kept Lipscomb united with his Northern brethren, despite their differences, until the last decade of the nineteenth century.

The extremists among the Disciples would attempt to effect a division in the Movement solely based upon one's belief about slavery. Campbell recognized that it was impossible to keep the extremists silent, so he urged Christians to remember their position of being guided only by the teachings of Scripture.

Campbell's pleas were soon overshadowed by a controversial episode involving a Disciple in Kansas named Pardee Butler, and the

Pardee Butler

American Christian Missionary Society. This was the first time that the abolitionists among the Disciples met the moderate Disciples in a head-to-head controversy.

Butler had taken his abolitionist views with him to Kansas in 1855. While preaching, Butler would habitually interject anti-slavery rhetoric. But the most substantial problem with Butler came in 1858 when he sought financial assistance from the ACMS.

An Ohio Disciple leader named Isaac Errett, was willing to financially help Butler, provided he abide by one stipulation, "It must, therefore, be distinctly understood, that if we embark in a missionary enterprise in Kansas, this question of slavery and anti-slavery must be ignored."

Butler, with his belief that slavery and Christianity were incompatible, would not accept such a condition. This spurred a fight with those Disciples who possessed a less extreme position when it came to slavery. However, it was not solely the abolitionists who incited division. There were several pro-slavery Disciples who were as equally passionate and uncompromising in their stance. One such man was James Shannon.

Shannon was the antithesis of Butler. He fervently believed that God created slavery, and, therefore, the institution was God-ordained. With such views, Shannon was the epitome of controversy. Yet, nothing he did was as controversial as a speech he delivered in 1855. The speech took place at a pro-slavery convention in Missouri. In a section of the stirring speech, Shannon called for war if the abolitionists would not adopt pro-slavery views.

James Shannon

But extremists like Butler and Shannon were tempered by moderate Disciples and, therefore, were unable to sever the Disciples' fellowship. What they did accomplish, though, was to cut a chink in the armor of unity based upon the Bible, which the Disciples so proudly wore.

The slavery issue provided a cause upon which the Northern and Southern Disciples could divide. And slavery was one of the issues that became an excuse for division.

Much like the controversy over the instrument, Lipscomb remained relatively silent on the slavery issue. His silence did not mean a lack of interest, but only pointed to a different focus. There was a greater question at hand for Lipscomb, and that was how the Christian relates to his government. His own personal transformation colored the words he wrote.

"The sword is divinely authorized, in the hand of the civil magistrate, for the vindication of right, the suppression of wrong."

— *Isaac Errett, 1863*

Brother Against Brother

The Issue of War and Pacifism

*P*erhaps as perplexing a question as that of the issue of slavery was the question of whether Christians should take part in the Civil War. Among the majority of Southern Disciple leadership was found a public commitment to pacifism and an earnest effort to protect the Movement from the divisive effects of the War.

In the North, however, was found a deep loyalty to the cause of the Union. It is interesting to note that Southern pacifists argued their position based upon religious convictions, while Northern participants took the same approach in arguing their position. The perception of the religious merits of each one's position played a crucial role in this controversy.

The dean of the Disciple leaders, Alexander Campbell, found himself in a difficult situation. He had entertained political leaders from the North and the South and had no wish to alienate the Disciples, based on geographical makeup. Yet, seventeen years previously, Campbell had made his views known on the subject in a speech he gave at Wheeling [West] Virginia, during the Mexican War in 1848, aptly called "An Address on War."

Without question, this address given by Campbell is the greatest argument for pacifism among the literature of the Disciples. However, a close second to Campbell's speech is David Lipscomb's *Civil Government*. While borrowing general ideas from Campbell's speech, Lipscomb molded a more detailed argument of the question. Like Campbell, he embraced the pacifist view. These works by Campbell and Lipscomb formed the basis for pacifist arguments among the Disciples.

The opinions of Campbell and Lipscomb were not accepted by all Disciples, though. Many wore the colors of the North and the South in the Civil War. Many found their loyalty to their home states or the geographical area in which they lived, as a greater impetus than pacifism. Not even the Disciples were immune from bearing arms against one another in a bitter political conflict. In short, the Civil War broke the ranks of the Disciples and cast a shadow over any chances of future unity.

In 1848, Campbell gave a stirring speech advocating pacifism. His arguments centered around the central authority of Jesus Christ for the Christian. Perhaps no Disciple's speech ever began with a more penetrating question: "Ladies and Gentlemen, has one Christian nation a right to wage war against another Christian nation?"[1]

The question was almost immediately dissected by Campbell as he argued that Christian nations do not wage war, at least by the orders of Christ, against one another. He based his argument on the fact that to use the word "Christian" one must assume that Christ is the head, since God has bestowed all authority on Christ. If Christ is the head, then that implies that any Christian nation belongs to him. In order to justify a Christian war, one must find his words of command or else it is not a justifiable war.

Recognizing the numerous accounts of war in the Old Testament, Campbell diffused any objections to his opinions by pointing out the special place of the Jews in history and the unique government under which they served. Campbell argued that the Jews received a divine command for their wars and obeyed the command because they worked within a theocracy which recognized God as the supreme leader.

As if anticipating objections to his comments, Campbell then made this bold challenge, "Let those, then, who now plead a jus divinum, a special divine warrant or right for carrying on war by the authority of the Lord Jesus Christ, produce a warrant from the present Monarch of the universe."[2]

If America, in light of its war with Mexico, was prone to declare that she, as God's people, was fighting a just war, Campbell simply called upon them to produce the evidence to support such an assertion. The main point for Campbell is that no war can be fought by Christians, except the war commissioned by the only one who has such authority: Jesus Christ.

Campbell did not merely deal with the collective argument of war, but he also addressed the issue of whether or not individual Christians may participate, in support of their government, in armed conflict. Often in conjunction with this question was the contention by Christians in support of armed conflict, that every Christian has a divine mandate to follow the orders of the "powers that be." Campbell's response was simply, "We cannot of right as Christian men obey the powers that be in anything not in itself justifiable by the written law of the great King—our liege Lord and Master, Jesus Christ."[3]

In surveying the wars fought throughout history, Campbell declared that none have served as "a process of justice" and not a single war "was such that an enlightened Christian man could have taken any part in it."[4] War simply was not morally acceptable according to Campbell. Rather, he thought that any dispute could be settled peaceably.

While Campbell's words in 1848 were meant to sway public opinion toward the moral stance of pacifism, he later urged neutrality among the Disciples, not for the purpose of protecting the country, but for preserving the already growing fragility of the Disciples. The Civil War frightened Campbell. In his 1848 speech he had spoken of the horrors of war. For Campbell, a greater horror would be the abandonment of the American Restoration Movement principles for a secular battle.

Even though Campbell strongly argued against Christian participation, he did not go as far as Lipscomb in arguing that the Christian must completely abstain from any political activity. Whereas Campbell believed Christians could hold public office, Lipscomb saw this as impossible in light of Campbell's arguments against any form of participation in wars.

Lipscomb was the most outspoken and influential of the Southern Disciple pacifists. The conservative leader took the pacifist position based on his understanding of the commandment: "Thou shalt not kill." For Lipscomb, the duty of the Christian was not to support the political position of his resident state, but rather, the duty of the Christian was to abstain from taking part in the conflict.[5]

Lipscomb's views were best articulated in a series of articles which he published in the *Gospel Advocate* and which afterward became a book entitled, *Civil Government.* In both of these instances, Lipscomb described three viewpoints concerning the relationship between civil government and the Christian. His first viewpoint was called the Roman Catholic view. In this view, the state and the church form an alliance for the benefit of each. Lipscomb's second view developed the idea of Protestantism. According to this view, Protestantism gave birth to rebellion in light of the corruption of the state. The third view, and the most agreeable to Lipscomb, was that the church and state should remain separate.[6]

To prove his point that Christians should not participate in war, Lipscomb sought to convince his readers that the origin of government is not God. He made the argument that civil government is of human origin. Lipscomb also believed that the creation of human government was a rejection of the government of God. As a result, human government will always be inefficient and will also bear the blame for the catastrophes with which humankind has had to deal. According to Lipscomb, wars take place because of "man's efforts to govern himself and the world."[7]

Lipscomb's pleas to Christians to abstain from participation in human government also was laced with an apocalyptic tone. Human governments (an invention of the devil according to Lipscomb), which God opposes will surely bring wrath not only on the organization, but also on the individual members of such organizations.[8]

A central feature of Lipscomb's arguments, as will later come in his argument against missionary societies and instrumental music in worship, was the silence of the Scriptures. This was the main reason, for Lipscomb, why Christians could not hold public office. He wrote, "The Christian's duty, as subject of earthly governments, is definitely revealed; but not a word, nor an example is given as to his duty, or the rules that should govern him as a manager or ruler in human government."[9]

Since the Bible unequivocally states that a person cannot serve two masters, Lipscomb concluded that Christians who participate in governmental affairs hurt the cause of Christ by not contributing their full talents and complete time to the cause of Christ. For Lipscomb, the conversion of the world to Christ superceded all other human objectives. He did not believe that the government could accomplish this or that the government was even divinely mandated to perform such activity. Rather, the task was God-given to the Church. Lipscomb believed that when Christians fulfill the mission which Christ has given them, then the problem of human governments will cease.

Like an Old Testament prophet, Lipscomb stated that all who initiate an armed conflict, who participate in such a conflict, and who support such action, are guilty of shedding innocent blood and directly disobeying God's command, "Thou shalt not kill."

Lipscomb's views on pacifism were his greatest and most controversial work. He drew the ire of Northern Unionists, Southern Confederates, and even those opposed to warfare. Lipscomb found himself virtually alone in the views he so strongly espoused.

Obviously, Lipscomb's pacifist views were not accepted by many Disciples. Sectional loyalty caused many Disciples to join Union or Confederate ranks and, then, take up arms against one another. The true importance of pacifism was seen not before or during the War, but in the years following this great conflict, for that is where Lipscomb first publicly voiced his opinions.

During the Civil War, Lipscomb had joined the majority of Disciple leaders in urging Christians to stay out of the conflict. His pleas echoed those in the *Gospel Advocate* by Tolbert Fanning. The *Advocate* editor did not take his pacifist views to the extreme that Lipscomb later did, but that did not stop him from preaching against involvement in the war. In the North, Benjamin Franklin, editor of the *American Christian Review*, preached pacifism as well. Unfortunately, his voice was a minority among the Northern Disciple leadership. Despite the others who pleaded for non-involvement, it was among these leaders in Tennessee that the strongest center of pacifism was found.

However, in addition to the voices in Tennessee and Indiana, there were also calls for pacifism among Disciples in the West. In 1861, fourteen leaders in Missouri signed a letter urging Disciples to remain neutral during the War. They saw no scriptural warrant to take up arms and no justification for joining the conflict.

> Whatever we may think of the propriety of bearing arms in extreme emergencies, we certainly can not, by the New Testament, which is our only rule of discipline, justify ourselves in engaging in the fraternal strife now raging in our beloved country.[10]

Campbell, always willing to print those articles in support of peace, published the letter in an issue of the *Millennial Harbinger*. However, Campbell refused to publish an article by one of the Movement's early leaders, Walter Scott. The first generation of leaders within the Restoration Movement was slowly making way for a new generation of leaders. Barton W. Stone had died in 1844. Thomas Campbell had died in 1854 and Walter Scott died at the beginning of the Civil War in 1861. Shortly before his death, however, Scott made his views known concerning the preservation of the Union. In an article he submitted to the *Harbinger*, Scott advocated the use of force to preserve the Union. "The government . . . that will not, with all its force, in defiance of all obstacles, put down anarchy and the doctrine that leads to it, ought itself to be put down."[11] Campbell refused to print the article. He felt that Scott's words were too controversial.

The marked difference between two of the early leaders of the Movement illustrates how deep the effects of sectionalism during the time and aftermath of the Civil War was on the Disciples. Never had they faced such a fierce enemy as the ones they called "brothers."

Many historians have discussed the question of whether or not the Disciples were divided by the Civil War. Philosophically speaking, it seems they were, but with no headquarters and no central government or leader practically-speaking, it is hard to see the division. Although the division was not clear, what is apparent is that the majority of the Disciples reacted from a sectional and not a Christian motivation.

Such a sectional reaction gives way to a theological, if not actual division. Without a central headquarters from which to issue any claims of severance, the task of proving that division took place becomes extremely difficult. Yet, in the immediate years after the Civil War, any doubt that two distinct groups had emerged among the Disciples was obvious. These were the years that Lipscomb wrote his articles on "Civil Government." These were also the years of the beginning of a new Disciple publication in the North: the *Christian Standard*, edited by Isaac Errett, who profoundly disagreed with the conclusions Lipscomb reached after the War.

Errett believed that the Christian had a divine duty to obey the governmental authorities. He also held the belief that some wars are justifiable. To Errett, the Civil War was necessary to put down what he saw as a Southern rebellion. In a sermon delivered in Detroit in 1863, Errett compared the obstinacy of the Confederacy with that of Rome in refusing to follow the laws of God. He then proceeded to say that no Southerner who called himself a Christian could justify the War.[12]

Isaac Errett

Errett, in contrast with Lipscomb, advocated the notion that God created civil government and the decisions of those authorities in this government must be obeyed by all—even the decision to engage in war. He said, "The sword is divinely authorized, in the hand of the civil magistrate, for the vindication of right, the suppression of wrong."[13]

This "divine authorization" argument carried immense weight in the decision of Disciple leaders to pass loyalty resolutions during the American Christian Missionary Society conventions in 1861 and 1863. These resolutions were the greatest Disciples' tragedy during the Civil War. One can only surmise the lesser extent that other issues would have had in dividing the Disciples if not for this crucial error in judgment. The tension created by the resolutions would still exist after the conclusion of the War. Those tensions served to embitter some Disciples against each other. The argument for pacifism inflamed the tension to even greater levels and served as a factor in the already-occurring division.

The primary issue of division was not church practice or church organization. The primary issue was the Christian's response to war. The previous four years had ripened the field for hostile discussions over the issue. And as would quickly become characteristic of the Movement, the Disciples did not shy away from controversy.

Many Disciples lost much during the War. Lipscomb himself endured the cruelty of Union and Confederate troops. The devastation wrought upon his beloved Tennessee had a deep impact on him and imbedded within him some hard feelings. But as far as formal division was concerned, Lipscomb was too much of a disciple of Campbell to seriously entertain such a notion—yet. There is no doubt that the devastation in the South was horrifying to a young Lipscomb. He, along with other Southern Disciples, could not escape the daily grim reminders of what the War had wrought.

The Civil War scarred Lipscomb deeply. He lost family members and possessions, and his grandmother's house was stripped of all its possessions by Union troops. These events further solidified Lipscomb's views that civil government has no relation to God's kingdom. American Restoration Movement historian Robert Hooper points out the transformation Lipscomb underwent because of the Civil War: "More than ever before, he realized that the only means of gaining Christian unity was to return completely to the New Testament as man's only guide. His optimism of the 1840s and 1850s was swept away by the ravages of the war."[14]

Other Disciples differed with Lipscomb's conclusions. Two

of them were James Garfield, who ascended to the Presidency of the United States in 1880, and Errett. In fact, it was a comment by Errett which pierced Lipscomb's soul the deepest. Writing in 1866, Errett, who had already grown tired of the discussion about pacifism wrote, "With many, this [pacifism] is a new-born faith, unknown before the recent civil war, and chiefly prevailing among those who were in sympathy with a lost cause."[15]

James Garfield

The words "lost cause" might have been the hardest for Lipscomb to read. The most important thing that he had lost during the War was not a breach of fellowship with other Disciples. It was not the possessions that were taken from his farm, and it was not even the deaths of relatives. The most important thing and what immensely strengthened his resolve to proclaim pacifism was the death of his only son, Zellner, in 1864. The child had become dehydrated and Lipscomb, because of the war conditions, could not get him the appropriate medical care. The child died June 26, 1864, only nine months old. When Lipscomb and his wife, Margaret, went to bury Zellner in a family cemetery, they had to pass through Union and Confederate check-points.[16] The fact that Lipscomb was unable to mourn the death of his son without governmental interference sheds some light on why he waged such a fierce battle against Christian participation in government. The government had waged a war, the benefits of which would never outweigh the loss experienced by Lipscomb.

Aside from the personal struggles of Lipscomb, the Disciples, as a whole, were still reeling from the effects of the War. Both those who participated in the War and those who had abstained from the effects of the War chided one another because each one believed his action was just. Hence, the post-war debate further inflamed the bitterness that was rapidly growing between Northern and Southern Disciples.

Moses Lard, an influential Northern Disciple leader, argued the case for pacifism in an 1866 article entitled, "Should Christians Go To War?' The article contained seven points in

Moses Lard

support of abstinence from armed combat. In leading up to his seven-fold argument, Lard raised two questions and made one statement. His first question was simply: " . . . does Christ permit his followers to fight therein?" To Lard, this was the crux of the matter. The second question Lard termed as "the issue." He wrote, "But does Christ permit a Christian to fight in any war? Not whether he may permit it; but whether he does permit it. This is the issue."[17]

Following his disclosure of what he saw as the issue, Lard then presented what he termed "the logical position." Lard wrote, "We do not affirm that no Christian can with Christ's approval fight in war; we deny that any can."[18]

Lard attempted "not to prove anything," but to show that those who argue that Christians may go to war "prove nothing" in their arguments. Lard took the stance that even a doubt concerning the morality of Christians fighting in battle settles the dispute.[19]

This doubt, and what Lard viewed as an indisputable argument against a Christian's involvement in war, led Lard to even suggest that it is better for a Christian to disobey his government than to take up arms, even if the government threatens retaliation.

Joining the prominent pacifists was J.W. McGarvey. The influential Kentucky leader, though in disagreement with Lipscomb over the Society question, agreed with the Nashville editor about pacifism. McGarvey urged Disciples to abstain from the conflict. He recognized, as the other pacifist leaders did, that this was not a Disciples' conflict. This was a conflict between temporal powers. The Disciples were fighting a spiritual battle. To

J. W. McGarvey

stray from the spiritual battle was to stray from the Movement's purpose. McGarvey argued that the "loyalty resolution" passed by the American Christian Missionary

Society in 1863 was such a case of the Disciples straying from a spiritual focus to a secular one.

The pacifistic hard line taken by Lipscomb, Lard and McGarvey found support among many Disciples but also raised serious questions for others. If their position was correct, then what is one to make of the decisions of Disciples like James A. Garfield to fight in the war? The answers would not come easily. In the years following the Civil War, the Disciples continued attempts at regaining the soul they lost in the bloody conflict known as the "War Between the States."

"We desire to put into the hands of every human being the Bible, without note or comment, that he may read in his own tongue the wonderful doings of God in creation, in providence, and redemption, and thereby become wise unto salvation."

— *D.S. Burnet, 1845*

Torn Asunder

The Missionary Society Controversy

Depending on how one views the American Christian Missionary Society, 1849 either was a year of great progress and development or it was a year that sparked the flames of division. Regardless of one's position, the birth of the ACMS remains as one of the most controversial acts within the history of the American Restoration Movement and one of the most influential.

David Staats Burnet

Yet, the idea was not without its precursors. Or to put it another way, behind every dream is a dreamer. The man responsible for the rise of national cooperative efforts among the Disciples was David Staats Burnet. Born in Ohio, in 1808, Burnet was reared in the Presbyterian faith. At an early age he decided to be immersed and joined the Baptist church. Such a change in faith indicates that Burnet was a deep thinker who truly sought to follow the Bible.

Burnet became acquainted with Alexander Campbell as early as 1827, when the two men traveled together. The influence of Campbell on Burnet was tremendous, for Burnet made strides toward the pursuit of primitive Christianity, at the same time Barton Stone, Walter Scott, and the Campbells were making the same move.

An indication of Burnet's move came when he served as the pastor of the Baptist Church in Dayton, Ohio. He led that congregation into a new era when the name was changed to the Central Church of Christ. The changes continued when in 1829, the church took a firm stand against creeds and made the decision to withdraw from the Baptist association of which it was a part.

As the Movement began to experience numerical growth, Burnet saw the potential of a national cooperative effort. His enthusiasm was sparked by a series of articles on church cooperation written by Campbell in the *Millennial Harbinger*. Burnet's dream was to establish a publishing house that would incorporate a missionary society. The purpose of this creation would be the distribution of the Bible. Burnet made his plea to the entire Movement through the pages of the *Millennial Harbinger*. He disclosed his motivation in the article, "We desire to put into the hands of every human being the Bible, without note or comment, that he may read in his own tongue the wonderful doings of God in creation, in providence, and redemption, and thereby become wise unto salvation."[1] Unfortunately, Burnet's vision did not end with the worldwide distribution of the Bible, nor the evangelization of the world.

Burnet's plea though, contained within the pages of Campbell's journal, did not receive the wholesale support of the influential editor. Interestingly, Campbell opposed this effort, but later served as the president of the ACMS. At first, Tolbert Fanning, who later vigorously opposed the ACMS, agreed to support Burnet's venture and served as one of the first vice presidents of the American Christian Bible Society.

Aylette Raines

The primary objections to the ACBS were outlined by Aylette Raines in an article in the *Millennial Harbinger*. Raines argued that no such society was needed given the already ongoing efforts of other denominations, such as the Baptists in 1837, to distribute the Bible. Because of these efforts, Raines saw no reason to begin a competing Bible society.

Campbell answered Burnet's impassioned plea for organization in the same issue of the *Millennial Harbinger* in a section entitled, "Remarks." Listing four points, Campbell argued that any such society must have the "support of the whole brotherhood." Campbell's next two points were centered on the relationship between Disciples and Baptists. He continued Raines' argument that the Baptists have already undertaken this venture. Campbell's third point was an attempt to not permanently sever relations with the Baptists. He argued that creating such a society would anger the Baptists. Instead of beginning a new organization, Campbell said that the Disciples should encourage the Baptists in their work.[2]

His fourth point was simply that the Disciples, in their current situation, did not have the membership or liberal giving that characterized the Baptists.

Several months later, the *Millennial Harbinger* contained Burnet's response to Campbell's statements. From the text of his article, it seems that Burnet was angered that Campbell, with whom he had agreed with on so many matters, now turned his back on this effort.

One of the stronger arguments made by Burnet was in regard to Campbell's assertion that any new organization must have the "support of the whole brotherhood." Burnet used this statement to take aim at one of Campbell's deepest passions: Bethany College, which he had founded. Burnet pointedly asked, "Was there a convention of the churches to establish Bethany College, the claims of which must now be heard, and until they are heard the Society must die in despair?"[3]

Burnet saw no difference in Campbell's initiative to establish a college and in his initiative to establish a society whose purpose was to distribute Bibles. To Burnet, Campbell was being hypocritical in his reasoning.

Burnet also took exception to Campbell's notion that such an endeavor would strain relations with the Baptists. In Burnet's mind, the new society would work in conjunction with the already established Baptist society. In fact, Burnet had already proposed the idea to the corresponding secretary of the Baptist society.[4]

The final argument that Burnet made was concerning Campbell's notion that the Movement did not have the membership nor the financial resources to sustain the new society. Burnet took this as Campbell's implying the brotherhood is "parsimonious."

As can be expected, Campbell wrote a lengthy reply immediately following Burnet's article. He accused Burnet of being "over-sensitive,"[5] and he also reiterated some of his previous statements and objections to the ABCS. Then he turned his attention to Burnet's claim that the establishment of Bethany College was no different from the establishment of a new society. In addressing this issue, Campbell argued against any parallel since Bethany College was not named American College. His point was that Burnet was attempting to form an entity that spoke for all and that is why Campbell argued he must have the "support of the whole brotherhood." In Campbell's mind a localized name for the society would have made the entire argument moot.

Following these comments, Campbell addressed the matter of cooperation with the Baptists. He was pleased with what Burnet reported in his previous article concerning the communication with the Baptist society, yet he still maintained that the Baptists would prefer cooperation rather than competition.

The dialogue between Campbell and Burnet was important in that it laid the foundation for the coming bitter discussion that would envelop the beginning and sustaining of the ACMS. This new society would develop from the enthusiasm and ardent desire of Disciples to introduce non-Christians to salvation in Christ via the effort to restore the "ancient order of things." The reality of this desire would be witnessed at the 1849 ACBS convention in Cincinnati.

The convention of 1849 was a time of excitement and curiosity among the Disciples. Doubtless, this was due to comments made by Campbell earlier in the year in the pages of the *Millennial Harbinger* desiring that some type of biblical organization be formed among the Disciples. Actually, Campbell had begun discussing church organization as early as 1841. In his days as editor of the *Christian Baptist*, he had vigorously opposed attempts at organizations via societies. But his views began to change during his editorship of the *Harbinger.* Campbell's position as one of the Movement's leaders, along with the respect that the Disciples had for him played a crucial role in the development of the missionary society and its promotion. Campbell's influence often muted criticism, but also led some to accept proposals too hastily.[6] Campbell's desire for church organization began to transform to reality when, on October 24, 1849, a Kentucky Disciple named John T. Johnson, proposed the creation of a national missionary society for the purpose of evangelizing the world.

At this time the Disciples were beginning to experience impressive growth, and not only did they believe they could turn the country to primitive Christianity, but they also believed the power of their message was so great that it had to be taken to foreign lands. The mindset of the Disciple leaders at this meeting prohibited them from seeing the risks of establishing such an organization.

Organizational efforts for the purpose of evangelism were nothing new to the congregations of the American Restoration Movement. For some years, several individual states had held cooperation meetings among congregations in their respective states. One such state was Tennessee. One of the primary forces behind the cooperation meetings was Tolbert Fanning, who orchestrated the first cooperation meeting in the state in 1842.

Fanning believed in the power of the simple gospel message. He also realized that for the Disciple churches in Tennessee to make a definitive mark in the state, there had to be intrastate church cooperation.

The first state cooperation meeting in Tennessee took place in 1842 in Nashville with twenty-nine churches represented. A variety of scriptural subjects were discussed and it was from this experience that Fanning developed a belief that much strife and bickering between churches could be avoided if brethren spent time together studying the Scriptures.

Fanning was enthused by these preliminary efforts and pondered the potential of the Disciples in Tennessee if some sort of cooperation was established. However, his pleas were largely unheeded by fellow Tennessee Disciples.

Since Fanning received little response he took the organizational task upon himself. His attempts began to produce results in the form of a greater interest by Tennessee churches and in the evolution of a state organization. The results blossomed following the 1847 meeting in the decision to make the church in Nashville a central point for evangelism through which all churches in the state could work.[7]

With this action, some churches began to express apprehension. At a meeting in Millersburg on September 11, 1847, the question of whether or not cooperation between churches is authorized by the Bible was raised. Fanning believed that the Scriptures authorized such cooperation and the majority of those at the Millersburg meeting took the same position. This was important, in light of Fanning's later opposition to the ACMS.

Fanning wrestled with the question of a national society. While leading efforts for a state society in Tennessee, he maintained a stressful relationship with the ACMS early on and severed his ties with the ACMS completely by the Civil War. However, Fanning did not immediately dismiss the ACMS. Instead, he waited to see what shape the ACMS took. He was named as one of the original twenty-nine vice presidents, but even from the beginning, his involvement in the Society was limited. His negative views of the Society would become further known a year after the creation of the ACMS, following the protest of the elders of a Disciples' church in Pennsylvania.

During the initial meeting of the ACMS in 1849 there was some discussion concerning the purpose of the organization. It was decided that it could be referred to as the American Christian Missionary Society. Some present thought this name, which was familiar with the ACBS, would engender support for this new cause. Even though not in attendance, Campbell was selected president of the new Society.

Campbell's leadership was certain to bring outbursts from those who had earlier been persuaded by his very own words, of the pitfalls of a missionary society; and who were now asked to support a missionary society with Campbell as its president. The consequences were obvious.

J. T. Barclay

Official incorporation for the ACMS did not occur until 1850. That year, the first foreign missionary commissioned by the Society, Dr. J.T. Barclay, was sent to Jerusalem to begin mission work. The year also witnessed the first congregational opposition to the Society.

Upon receiving the new Society's constitution in the mail, the elders at the Church of Christ in Connellsville, Pennsylvania, called a meeting to discuss this new organization. They concluded that such an organization was unscriptural and prone to cause division. They detailed their position by listing ten resolutions and sent a letter containing these ten resolutions to four Disciple journals, one of which was the *Millennial Harbinger.*

The ten resolutions read as follows:

1st   That we deem it the duty of every Christian, to do all within his power for the advancement of the cause of Christ, by holding forth the Word of Life to the lost and ruined man.

2nd   That we consider the Church of Jesus Christ, in virtue of the commission given her by our blessed Lord, the only scriptural organization on earth for the conversion of sinners and sanctification of believers.

3rd   That we, as members of the body of Christ, are desirous of contributing, according to our ability, for the promulgation of the gospel in foreign lands; but

4th   That, conscientiously, we can neither aid nor sanction any society, for this or other purposes, apart from the church, much less one which would exclude from its membership many of our brethren, and all of the apostles, if now upon the earth, because silver and gold they had not.

5th   That we consider the introduction of all such societies a dangerous precedent—a departure from the principles for which we have always contended as sanctioning the chapter of expediency—the evil and pernicious efforts of which the past history of the church proves.

6th That we also consider them necessarily heretical and schismatical, as much so as human creeds and confessions of faith, when made the bonds of union and communion.

7th That for missions, both foreign and domestic, we approve of a plan similar to that adopted by the brethren of Tennessee, for evangelizing the State.

8th That we consider it the duty of all the churches to cooperate in home missions, and that we are willing and ready to unite with those of Western Pennsylvania, in sustaining evangelists to proclaim the gospel in destitute places.

9th That we highly approve of a new and pure translation of the Holy Scriptures, both for home and foreign uses.

10th That a copy of these resolutions be sent, for publication, to the *Millennial Harbinger, Christian Age, Christian Magazine, and the Proclamation and Reformer.*[8]

These ten resolutions incorporated the first congregational-wide challenge to the ACMS. It is interesting to note the emphasis in several of the resolutions. One essential point for the Connellsville elders was the absence of a "Thus saith the Lord" for the creation of the missionary society. In their reasoning, Christ had established the church and had given her a divine mandate to "preach the gospel and make disciples of all nations." Therefore, the church is the only missionary society authorized by the Bible. Secondly, they refused to violate their consciences in the matter. This point was made in the fourth resolution.

The fifth and sixth resolutions contain the harshest criticism of the ACMS. In these two resolutions the elders argued that a dangerous precedent had been set, because such a society abandoned a key aspect of the nature of the Movement. The necessity of membership, and paid membership dues at that, rendered, in their minds, the Society schismatical.

Also interesting was the elders' hearty approval to the cooperation efforts that were taking place in Tennessee. To the

Connellsville elders, this situation was more in tune with the scriptural examples of church cooperation. On making this point, the elders explicitly welcomed the opportunity for cooperative efforts with other Disciple congregations in Western Pennsylvania.

At the very least, the resolutions are captivating. The elders seemed to have followed the example of Thomas Campbell, specifically, his words in the *Declaration and Address*, and had determined, as he did, that any such innovation would bring with it division. In addition to the Bible and the words of the elder Campbell, they also had the words of Walter Scott who addressed the matter of church cooperation in an article in the *Christian Messenger* in 1827. Even though Scott wrote in support of church cooperation and conventions, the points he made were different from those contained within the constitution of the ACMS.

Barton Stone responded to Scott's article, agreeing with the thrust of Scott's argument, but pointed out that such organization can easily become tyrannical.[9]

Stone's insight illuminated the real concern of the Connellsville elders. They, along with most other Disciples, did not wish the Movement to adopt any system or organization which contained a hierarchical chain-of-command. The Society faced its first significant challenge.

Campbell answered the challenge of the Connellsville elders by writing that those involved in the establishment of the ACMS "anticipated" differences of opinion among the Disciples. As a result, Campbell pleaded with the Connellsville elders to be patient.

During this time a young farmer turned preacher in Tennessee, named David Lipscomb observed, from a distance, what was happening within the brotherhood. Yet, he would not take an active role in the Society debate until 1863.

Despite no direct involvement in the creation of the Society, Lipscomb still was a participant through his relationship with his older brother, William Lipscomb and mentor, Tolbert Fanning.

Fanning, who saw the direction in which the Movement seemed to be heading, namely, the emphasis on the efforts and activities of Northern Disciples, decided to, along with William Lipscomb, launch a new publication. The title of the new journal was the *Gospel Advocate*. The name went hand-in-hand with its purpose of advocating the gospel of Jesus Christ. The initial aim of the publication was to be a journal for all the congregations in the Movement. However, the *Gospel Advocate* evolved into the voice of the Southern Disciples. More than that, it became the voice of the conservative Southern Disciples.

"Should we ever meet them in the flesh, can we fraternize with them as brethren? How can the servants of the Lord of this section ever strike hands with the men who now seek their life's blood?"

— *Tolbert Fanning, 1861*

Sectionalism

The Effect of the ACMS Loyalty Resolutions

As if the Civil War was not a dangerous enough threat of division among the Disciple ranks, the actions of the American Christian Missionary Society in 1861 and 1863 created a rift that would never be repaired.

One of the claims of the majority of Restoration Movement historians, as well as some of the leaders at the time, was that the Disciples remained united throughout the Civil War. Such an assertion, however, disregards the lasting effect of the "loyalty resolutions" proposed and passed at ACMS conventions in 1861 and 1863.

Without question, the Civil War was fought by a deeply divided country. The Ohio River was not the only mark of division between North and South. Slavery was an issue constantly debated during this time. Also debated was the concept of a centralized government in relation to individual states' rights. These issues, slavery in particular, had already divided the largest religious denominations in the country. The leaders among the Disciples struggled to maintain the unity of the Movement. Their efforts were greatly complicated in 1861.

In October, 1861, the ACMS held its national convention in Cincinnati. One obvious peculiarity about this meeting was the fact that not a single Disciples leader from the Deep South was in attendance. Another interesting fact was the number of church leaders from the North came to the convention wearing Union soldier uniforms.

A resolution was proposed by an Ohio Disciple named Dr.

J.P. Robinson. The resolution was seconded by L.L. Pinkerton, minister for the Midway, Kentucky, church.

This proposed resolution read:

> Resolved, that we deeply sympathize with the loyal and patriotic in our country, in the present efforts to sustain the Government of the United States. And we feel it our duty as Christians, to ask our brethren everywhere to do all in their power to sustain the proper constitutional authorities of the Union.[1]

Questioned by D.S. Burnet, this resolution was ruled germane to the interests of the ACMS by Isaac Errett. In fact, the matter was not germane, according to the original constitution of the ACMS. The second article states the purpose of the Society: "The object of this Society shall be to promote the spread of the gospel in destitute place of our own and foreign lands."[2]

It seems that Errett found himself caught in a difficult position. He saw how the slavery debate was causing division among the Disciples and had struggled to keep the ACMS from passing any resolutions concerning the slavery question. However, he felt that he could prevent an official resolution concerning slavery as well as prevent a loyalty resolution to the Union.

Years after the passing of the "loyalty resolutions," Errett's biographer, J.S. Lamar, candidly wrote,

> Of course everybody understands now that the action was unauthorized by the organized law of the Society; that it had no connection, immediate or remote, with its true purposes and objects; and that, being ultra vires, it was wholly illegitimate and unwarranted.[3]

J. S. Lamar

Errett hoped to prevent division in the Movement, but this action forever colored him in the minds of Southern Disciples.

Such an action was foreign to the ACMS conventions. The unprecedented resolution came despite the efforts of leaders to prevent such a resolution from a vote. Raccoon John Smith was one of the leaders who raised an objection to the resolution, but rescinded his objection after sharp debate. The objection was raised a third time, and this time it was decided that the matter was not germane to the Society. A ten-minute recess was called. During this recess a "mass meeting" was hastily organized. The original "loyalty resolution" was reintroduced and passed with one dissenting vote. Those present thought this strategy would enable the Society to continue to function by holding an official "neutral" position in regard to the Civil War. However, the men who voted had no authority to pass such a resolution.

Interestingly, James A. Garfield, a colonel in the Union army, gave a short speech preceding the adoption of the resolution. What part the friendship between Errett and Garfield played in this disastrous occurrence cannot officially be known. What is known, however, is that Southern Disciples from this point on viewed any cause or idea associated with Errett or Garfield with suspicion. The rift between North and South had widened. Some even called the resolution, since the meeting took place in Cincinnati, as the "Ohio Point of View."[4]

Following the lead of the ACMS, the Indiana State Missionary Society passed a loyalty resolution the next year. This action brought a heated response by Benjamin Franklin. Not only was Franklin the editor of the influential *American Christian Review*, but he was also a supporter of the ACMS.

Franklin's critical remarks about the state society's actions prompted a rebuttal by another Indiana Disciple named Elijah Goodwin. Goodwin felt that Franklin was attempting to cause a "schism." Franklin did not wish to make a schism, but he did realize that his views concerning the Missionary Society were changing. What made Franklin move from support of the Society to opposition is not known. One possibility is that Franklin realized the wrongs committed by the ACMS in 1861. Many found it difficult to reconcile the fact that an organization committed to evangelism would delve into politics and attempt to pass a binding resolution on the brotherhood, no matter how "unofficial" such action was. Another reason, which would not be apparent until 1866, was Franklin's bitterness over the beginning of the *Christian Standard*. Franklin realized that this new publication would compete for his readers and he also realized that the men behind the start of the *Standard* were unimpressed and somewhat irritated by his conservative views.

The passing of the resolution immediately alienated brethren in the South, and brought a swift and harsh reaction. Fanning wrote that by making such a resolution the Northern Disciple leaders were "approving most heartily the wholesale murder of people South who do not chose [sic] to be governed by a sectional party North."[5]

Fanning also alluded to the fact that the actions of the members of the ACMS hindered the unity of the Movement, and could, quite possibly, cause its division. "Should we ever meet them in the flesh, can we fraternize with them as brethren? How can the servants of the Lord of this section ever strike hands with the men who now seek their life's blood?"[6] The action also severely put the Southern leaders in a difficult situation. Already the leaders were faced with trying to keep the unity of the Movement intact with those sympathetic and those committed to the Confederate cause. They found this much more difficult following the Society's affirmation of the "loyalty resolution" in 1863.

Lipscomb left no doubt of his opinion about the action of the ACMS when he wrote that the "Society committed a great wrong against the Church and cause of God."[7]

Lipscomb was grieved because the "loyalty resolutions" further complicated the position with which he was struggling. He wanted the preservation of the Union, but as a Southerner, his loyalties also laid with the South. In spite of all this, he still remained ardently opposed to any involvement, on the part of Christians, in the affairs of government. Clearly, though, Lipscomb's foremost goal was the preservation of the Disciples. His commitment to unity is a trait that characterized his life. Lipscomb would recognize division, but not breach of fellowship.

Not only did the Society's actions adversely affect Lipscomb, but they also deeply affected Franklin, who through this experience solidified a position in opposition to missionary societies.

Franklin's turnaround was also possibly influenced by a meeting with Fanning at Franklin College in which the two men discussed the Society question at length. According to one account, " . . . when Franklin left Fanning, he offered him his right hand as a pledge to join his resistance to the societies."[8]

Supposedly, an article that appeared in the *Christian Pioneer*, stating that "every preacher of note" had taken an anti-war position, was the motivation for Northern, pro-Union Disciple leaders to pass the "loyalty resolution." The evidence for this is found in a letter sent to the *Christian Pioneer*, simply signed, "One of the Men."[9]

Unfortunately, the tension created from the 1861 convention grew even greater when the ACMS convened again in 1863. Apparently, some of the Society members were not satisfied with the 1861 resolution. Now the ACMS members considered a series of loyalty resolutions, introduced by Randall Faurot, of a much stronger language.

The effects of the Civil War along with the growing sectional bitterness among the Disciples were partially to blame for this new action. The animosities already present between Northern and Southern Disciples were heightened by the series of resolutions made in 1863.

After the meeting was called to order by Burnet, the series of resolutions were introduced. They read as follows:

> Whereas, "there is no power but of God," and "the powers that be are ordained of God;" and whereas, we are commanded in the Holy Scriptures to be subject to the powers that be, and "obey magistrates," and whereas an armed rebellion exists in our country, subversive of these divine injunctions; and whereas, reports have gone abroad that we, as a religious body, and particularly as a Missionary Society, are to a certain degree disloyal to the Government of the United States; therefore –
>
> Resolved, That we unqualifiedly declare our allegiance to said Government, and repudiate as false and slanderous any statements to the contrary.

Resolved, That we tender our sympathies to our brave and noble soldiers in the fields, who are defending us from the attempts of armed traitors to overthrow the Government, and also to those bereaved, and rendered desolate by the ravages of war.

Resolved, That we will earnestly and constantly pray to God to give our legislators and rulers, wisdom to enact, and power to execute, such laws are [as] will speedily bring to us the enjoyment of a peace that God will design and bless.[10]

This time, however, Errett declared, to no avail, that these new resolutions were not germane to the Society's interests. After a motion to adjourn was dismissed, the convention voted to adopt the new resolutions.

Using such a terms as "armed traitors" to describe Confederate soldiers, including Disciples who fought for the Confederacy, cut a deep wound in the heart of Southern Disciple leaders.

The affirming of the resolutions drew the ire of J.W. McGarvey, the noted Disciples leader in Kentucky who would later serve on the faculty of the College of the Bible in Lexington. McGarvey had defended the Society against its critics. Although opposed to the introduction of the instrument in the worship assembly, McGarvey believed wholeheartedly in the ACMS and in its goal of evangelizing the world. However, McGarvey, along with many others, recognized the disastrous effects the 1863 resolutions would have on the Movement. The Southern Disciples still had bitter feelings over the 1861 "loyalty resolution." Now the new series of resolutions, which negatively referred to Disciples who sided with the Confederacy, could do nothing but more harm. McGarvey's anger toward the ACMS is evidenced by this pronouncement: "I have judged the American Christian Missionary Society, and have decided for myself, that it should now cease to exist."[11]

The immediate problems that occurred as a result of the loyalty resolutions of 1861 and 1863 did not have to happen. The reason for the existence of the ACMS was not to enter into the political arena. The ACMS was an effort to pool the growing resources of the Disciples for the cause of evangelizing the world. The Disciples had begun to experience significant growth and with that growth came the dreams of uniting a divided Christendom and leading the world into the salvation offered through Jesus Christ. The ACMS actions destroyed both those possibilities.

However, the ACMS convention in 1862 made no forays into politics or loyalty resolutions. There were, though, some harsh words exchanged between McGarvey and Burnet concerning the language of a report given by Burnet which referred to the "rebellion."[12]

McGarvey continued to express his frustration in a report, approved by the Kentucky State Missionary Society, which took exception with Kentucky Disciples who had chosen to take up arms. As can be imagined, with the large number of Disciples committed to the Union in attendance, McGarvey's comments were not accepted. In fact, Elijah Goodwin countered by making public a report that commended "those faithful brethren" who were fighting on behalf of the Union cause, and therefore, choosing to "be subject to the powers that be."[13]

William Pendleton

Attempts to undo the damage done by the 1863 proposal were abundant. The son-in-law of Alexander Campbell, William K. Pendleton, made these comments in the *Millennial Harbinger* in 1864:

It ought not to be disguised, that the fortunes of the American Christian Missionary Society have for a year or two been under a cloud. The confidence of many of her oldest and most liberal supporters has been in good measure withdrawn from her, and she has not been repaid for this loss by a correspondent accession of new friends. Doubtless many extravagant representations both of the things that were done and of the spirit in which they were urged, have been made, yet the fact that the Society violated her constitution, in introducing and forcing to a willful vote a set of political resolutions, cannot be denied or explained away.[14]

The loyalty resolutions of 1861 and 1863, while not dictating doctrine, did dictate policy. To a majority of the members of the Society the churches in the Restoration Movement had to support the Union because the Union's cause was the just one. Southern Disciples rejected such a notion, because they strongly felt that their cause was the morally superior one.

In the end, political leanings caused severe damage to the fragile unity that was at the center of the American Restoration Movement.

Of course, in light of the events to come, such a claim is an understatement.

"I do not mean to affirm that the Bible contains a fully developed scheme of Missionary operations. It is not at all necessary that it should. It is enough that it develops the essential principles of such a scheme."

— *Robert Milligan, 1866*

Brothers at Odds

Division Moves Closer to Reality

The one Northern activity that drew the most ire from Lipscomb was the American Christian Missionary Society. Lipscomb believed that anything that contributed to the Society should be opposed, even something as apparently harmless as a new hymnal published by the Society. In examining Lipscomb's attitude it becomes obvious that the loyalty resolutions of 1861 and 1863 had left a deep scar on the Southern leader. One benefit the scar had, though, was that Lipscomb could relate to the struggles of the Southern Disciples. He had experienced firsthand the devastation in the South because of the war and intimately knew the struggle of the average Southerner to recover from the epic conflict. The loyalty resolutions, in Lipscomb's mind, had advocated the shedding of the blood of Southern Disciples fighting in behalf of their home states.

In addition to the fact that the new Society-published hymnal would financially help the Society, Lipscomb also disliked the updating of the language of some of the hymns and believed the hymnal was designed for city churches. However, these were only symptoms of Lipscomb's true opposition. For Lipscomb, anything that contributed to the Society should be opposed.

In all fairness, though, Lipscomb did travel to Cincinnati to meet with the publisher of the new hymnal, H.S. Bosworth in

June, 1866. The meeting did nothing to change Lipscomb's feelings on the matter.[1]

Lipscomb did not merely criticize, though. Realizing that the publication of the new hymnal would take place regardless of his criticism, he made plans to publish the old hymnal in Canada.[2]

This minor hymnal controversy foreshadowed the coming of a greater hymnal controversy in the 1880s. In this second controversy, bitter words were exchanged between Lipscomb and Isaac Errett, editor of the Northern-based, *Christian Standard*. The gap between Northern and Southern Disciples continued to widen.

The surrender of Confederate General Robert E. Lee to Union General Ulysses S. Grant at Appomattox Court House in Virginia signaled the end of the bloodiest conflict in United States history. Unfortunately, the end of the war did not mark the end of the Society controversy. If the end of the Civil War did anything in relation to the differences of opinion over the ACMS, it afforded more time for the Disciples to wage their verbal warfare.

The current state of the Society was also in disarray. Incoming funds had declined and the few attempts at foreign missions had proved less than successful. Originally, the ACMS had focused on foreign evangelism, but because of the Society's lack of success and the rapid population growth of the nation, the Society changed its focus to domestic missions.[3]

This change of focus increased the volume of anti-society rhetoric. Men like Fanning and Lipscomb, who saw the good accomplished in intrastate church cooperation, could not understand why a national society was needed. Then again, after the War, most Southerners shuddered at the notion of a centralized government's powers superseding the rights of individual states. The decline of funds and interest among Disciples proved that the brotherhood was having a difficult time justifying the existence of the ACMS.

To calm the rising tide of opposition, a new pro-society journal named the *Christian Standard* was begun. Isaac Errett served as the editor and the new periodical focused on promoting the continued support and existence of the Society.

The creation of this new journal with Errett as editor did not bode well for the fragile unity of the Movement. Already, Lipscomb and Errett had clashed over the Society hymnal and now the two men had taken opposing sides in what would become the two most influential journals among the Disciples.

There was no doubt of the strained relationship between Errett and Lipscomb. The founders of the *Christian Standard* believed their publication was necessary to represent the heart of the Movement. They thought that the *Gospel Advocate* and the *American Christian Review* (edited by Benjamin Franklin) were too "narrow in their views on Scriptural truth, essentially sectarian in spirit, and, hurtful rather than helpful to the great cause which they assumed to represent."[4]

The *Standard* gave much needed support to the Society, but it also provided more fuel for the continual bickering about national cooperation. Opponents were not silenced with the advent of the *Standard*.

Out of the arguments against the Society arose four main points:

1. the selling of memberships,

2. the fact there was no divine mandate for the creation of societies,

3. the attempt to replace the local church as the scripturally-ordained missionary society, and

4. because of the three points already listed, a belief that since the church embodied the divine method for evangelizing the world, to establish, advocate and support the para-church missionary societies were heretical and schematic.[5]

Proponents of the Society quickly counterattacked by arguing for expediency and the freedom of the church to act where the Scriptures were silent. They also argued that "missionary societies were allowing the churches to fulfill the Great Commission while the anti-society position of the opponent actually prevented them from fulfilling the last command of Jesus Christ."[6]

Robert Milligan

The defense of the ACMS culminated in an article by Robert Milligan, which appeared in an 1866 issue of the *Christian Standard.* In this article, Milligan outlined thirteen theses in defense of the Society. Milligan argued that cooperation must take place, because as each church is a missionary society, so is the denomination to which the churches belong. Milligan continued his defense of the Society by arguing that there is no need for an explicit Scriptural command in such matters. He wrote, "I do not mean to affirm that the Bible contains a fully developed scheme of Missionary operations. It is not at all necessary that it should. It is enough that it develops the essential principles of such a scheme."[7]

Milligan's argument concerning the relationship of the church and a national missionary society was opposed by Robert Richardson. A year later Richardson wrote, "Is it true, then, that the Church is already organized with a view to missionary labor? If it be, then certainly nothing more is needed, and the controversy is at an end." However, the controversy was far from settled in Richardson's mind. "It is entirely a mistake to suppose that the Church is already organized for missionary work. The truth is, however strangely it may sound to some, that the Church is not organized at all for any purpose whatever."[8]

Tolbert Fanning was not persuaded. In addition to the argument that the missionary society is unscriptural, Fanning also took particular exception to the expediency argument. Since resuming publication of the *Gospel Advocate* following the Civil War, Lipscomb and Fanning had been questioned as to what position the *Advocate* would take in regard to the ACMS. Clearly, Disciples were taking sides on the issue.

Lipscomb and Fanning had determined to address the issue of cooperation and organizations at first, but did not understand why Disciples would base their support of the *Advocate* on the journal's relationship to the ACMS. It seems that both Fanning and Lipscomb had accepted the existence of the

Society, despite their opposition, and now sought to publish a journal for their Southern Disciple brethren. However, this did not mean that the men would never remark about the Society again. In fact, Fanning wrote, "Indeed, a chief purpose we had in view in establishing 'The Gospel Advocate,' was to examine the subjects of 'Christian co-operation,' 'Church organization,' the classes and qualifications of officers in the body, and especially, the worship of the saints, public and private."[9]

Since the opposition against the Society had escalated and the charitable funds received had declined, the Society was forced to take action. The result was the Louisville Plan.

Officially adopted in 1869, the Louisville Plan was the result of a twenty-member committee, commissioned in 1868, to formulate a working plan, which would not only appeal to those in opposition to the Society, but would also increase congregational support. Presented by William T. Moore, the plan was a highly detailed and somewhat confusing effort that, if successful, would give more control to local congregations. The thrust of the plan was this: delegates were to be appointed by local congregations to represent them at district conventions. From these conventions delegates were appointed to attend the state convention. And from the state convention, two delegates were selected to attend the national convention. To ensure that proper representation was made, the plan called that for every 5,000 Disciples in the state, there must be one delegate.

The financial aspects of the Louisville Plan were no less confusing. In essence, individual congregations raised missionary funds. This money would then go to the treasurer of the district, from which it was equally divided between state and district mission work. Out of the money sent to the state society, half then went to the General Missionary Convention.[10] By this time, the ACMS had become an organism operating within a larger organization.

In terms of brotherhood acceptance, the most important member of the committee which devised the plan was Franklin. His approval was crucial. Yet, not even the blessing of Franklin could persuade Lipscomb. The Louisville Plan was still a system for mission work that superceded the local church. As such, Lipscomb could never approve of it.

However, Lipscomb would not have long to oppose the effort, because in 1875, the plan was dissolved after basically floundering in its only year of existence. To Lipscomb's dismay, another organizational attempt followed the demise of the Louisville Plan. In the midst of the years of the Louisville Plan, Lipscomb posed a question that later made him sound like a prophet: "How shall Christian unity be maintained?" His conclusion, after remarking of the changes he saw taking shape in the Movement was that the threat of division was quickly becoming reality.

Lipscomb stood alone after the death of Fanning in 1874. The man from whom he had learned so much and from whose reasoning he adopted various beliefs, his mentor, was gone. Lipscomb was now seen as the primary voice of the Southern Disciples, and the primary voice of the conservative Disciples. Franklin was nearing the end of his life and would die in 1878, thus leaving the conservative mantle to Lipscomb, although a brash Indiana Disciple named Daniel Sommer would claim to carry on Franklin's legacy.

In closing this chapter on the place of the missionary society in the division of the Disciples, it is pertinent to comment on another sad chapter in American Restoration Movement history: the fallout between Lipscomb and McGarvey. This episode, occurring between two powerful conservative leaders, would prove Robert Hooper's assertion that "The missionary society was the most divisive issue with the Restoration Movement . . . It is the one thing that divided the more conservative elements of the disciples."[11] Nowhere is this assertion more clearly seen than in the bitter conflict between Lipscomb and McGarvey.

The one issue that most clearly defined the tension between Lipscomb and McGarvey was the missionary society. Take away this issue and the men agreed virtually on every other matter. The only difference was McGarvey's willingness to fellowship with those he believed were in error.[12] It is unfortunate that a difference of opinion concerning one issue could prohibit a close friendship and working relationship between two great leaders of the Movement. One could argue that Stone and Campbell could have overcome such a difference in order to work hand-in-hand. But, Lipscomb and McGarvey were not Stone and Campbell. Such was an example of the difference in first and second generation leadership among the Disciples.

The Society issue hit closer to home for Lipscomb when Tennessee Disciples met in Chattanooga in 1890 to form a state missionary society. Lipscomb attended the meeting and presented his reasons as to why such an organization was unscriptural. Despite being granted the opportunity to speak against the organization, Lipscomb could not persuade those present to abandon such a notion. How Lipscomb must have wished that Fanning was still alive.

Naturally, the *Advocate* spoke out against the new organization, while the *Standard* commended such an effort. Another powerful journal at the time, the *Christian-Evangelist*, also wrote favorably of the action. This journal was edited by J. H. Garrison and was seen as the most progressive of the three publications.

Lipscomb was dismayed at this course of events and used his strongest language yet in condemning this action. To Lipscomb, these Tennessee Disciples were being led astray by a few pro-society brethren.[13]

His language was blunt and unmistakable when he used the phrase "the invention of the devil" to describe the missionary society.[14] Such terminology was bound to elicit response from those in favor of the Society. The response, though, came in the form of scheduling rather than a prolonged debate in the *Advocate*. The General Convention of the ACMS took place in Nashville in 1892. Those who had sided with Lipscomb on the Society question were furious and made plans for another convention to take place in Nashville during the General Convention. Lipscomb resisted such a carnal response. But Lipscomb could not dispel the notion that the holding of the Convention in Nashville was a deliberate slap-in-the-face to those opposing the Society.[15]

What Lipscomb needed was a nationally-known and respected Disciples' leader to stand with him in the opposition to the missionary society. Based on his conservatism, McGarvey was the logical person to do so. McGarvey was conservative, and opposed innovations in the church, except for the Society, which he supported wholeheartedly. McGarvey's opposition of innovations, in particular the use of the instrument in worship, and his support of the missionary society was something that Lipscomb could never reconcile in his own thinking. This seeming inconsistency also was questioned by Garrison in the pages of the *Christian-Evangelist*.[16]

Though agreeing on so many issues, Lipscomb and McGarvey's relationship was cordial at best. Though on certain occasions, McGarvey threw out any notion of tact, especially when he desired to make a point in his writing. One reason for this is that "he made no distinction between the man and his teaching."[17]

In 1869, McGarvey even attacked Lipscomb personally by making fun of his preaching style and ability. Such criticism may have been generated from criticism that Lipscomb had earlier made in reference to the school where McGarvey taught, the College of the Bible. In 1891, Lipscomb had begun the Nashville Bible School, which had the purpose of training men to be preachers. McGarvey could not pass on this golden opportunity to retaliate. "If awkwardness is necessary in order to preach to the poor, we think many of them (students at Lipscomb's school) would do well to go out preaching with Bro. Lipscomb himself."

Lipscomb, obviously hurt by such a personal attack, responded, "Why Bro. McGarvey should have this personal thrust at my misfortune I do not know."[18]

The attempts to reconcile the two men were unsuccessful. Even T. B. Larimore, the stirring Alabama preacher, attempted to bridge the gap, but to no avail. Larimore was always one to seek common ground, for he believed

T. B. Larimore

that the Disciples' primary purpose was to

preach the Gospel. Not prone to getting into disputes about the swirling issues of the day, Larimore realized the good that could be accomplished if Lipscomb and McGarvey would lay aside their differences. Unfortunately, that action never came.

While the missionary society was not functioning as desired and its critics still loudly protesting, McGarvey wrote an article for the *Christian Standard* exhorting brethren to stand united in the cause of evangelism and find a compromise in their differing opinions about the missionary society. A sense of urgency filled the air as Disciples clamored to find a way to remain united. This was complicated by the fact that two years previously Daniel Sommer had stirred up 6,000 Indiana Disciples to draw specific lines of fellowship in regard to those Disciples who supported innovations such as the Society.

McGarvey's compromise was based upon the financial aspects of the Society. In his compromise he called for a deeper look at the scriptural authorization of societies and for the cessation of fundraising on the part of missionary societies. "McGarvey's compromise called on everyone to allow the freedom to band together in para-church organizations but that such organizations had no inherent right to other people's money."[19] McGarvey believed that if minor changes in the system could be made, then division could be averted. McGarvey failed to realize that division had already come.

As can be expected, Disciples on both sides of the missionary society question responded negatively to the compromise. Neither side felt McGarvey had gone far enough in his arguments. Lipscomb was one of those men. He still could not look past the fact that an unscriptural organization and not the local church, would "control" the missionary.[20]

The verbal sparring between Lipscomb and McGarvey over the "society question" continued for several years since each man was unwilling to budge. However, Lipscomb never lost respect for McGarvey. He viewed him as a scholar and an asset to the cause of the Disciples. That admiration was a one-way street. Historian Robert Hooper tells an interesting story to illustrate this point. F. D. Srygley, future editor of the *Advocate*, remarked to McGarvey in the late 1890's, that he should have exhibited some gratitude to Lipscomb. McGarvey, being for the society and against the instrument, found himself in an awkward position. Most churches were for both the society and the instrument or were against both the society and the instrument. Srygley pointed out that Lipscomb, along with the *Advocate*, had provided "churches where he (McGarvey) might hold membership and preach." McGarvey, in characteristic fashion responded that "many churches existed that had neither heard of Lipscomb . . . nor had ever read a copy of the *Gospel Advocate.*" Unsatisfied with his reply, McGarvey ended his statement with a particularly vicious attack on Lipscomb by comparing the editor with a fly: "A fly, sitting on the rear end of a stagecoach and looking back, exclaimed, 'See what a dust we are a kicking up!'"[21]

Lipscomb remained steadfast in his admiration of McGarvey, but sadly the two men would never completely unite in their endeavors. One wonders what effect the union of these two influential men could have had on the next several tumultuous years. However, one does not have to wonder about the effect their division had. The ramifications of such division have been discussed for years and have caused some historians of the Movement to draw dramatic conclusions, as does Leroy Garrett when he surmises, "The difference between Lipscomb and McGarvey provides us with a bottom line on how and why the Church of Christ emerged."[22]

"In the early years of the present Reformation, there was entire unanimity in the rejection of instrumental music from our public worship."

— J.W. McGarvey, 1864

The Effect of Silence on Worship:

The Instrumental Music Debate

During the years of the ACMS, debate arose over another controversial issue that would further widen the division taking place among the Disciples. Although overshadowed by the "society question" until the 1870s, the issue of instrumental music in worship etched its place in Restoration Movement history by polarizing leaders who agreed with Thomas Campbell's dictum, "Where the Scriptures speak, we speak; where the Scriptures are silent, we are silent," but differed as to the motto's interpretation.

However, the introduction of the instrument was not simply about biblical interpretation (hermeneutics). It was also symptomatic of the growing wedge between Northern and Southern culture in light of the reconstruction efforts following the Civil War. Seen in this light, the instrument further fostered sectionalism, and therefore, contributed mightily to the division of the Movement.

As witnessed in the preceding chapter, the question as to the scriptural authority of the missionary society was not resolved. Positions were held firmly, except in the case when Benjamin Franklin reversed his position following the loyalty resolutions. The result was a widening gap between the Disciples.

Before proceeding with a telling of the events surrounding the introduction and debate over the use of the instrument in worship, it is important to understand that neither the American Christian Missionary Society nor the instrument were the causes of division. The main question centered on how a person interprets the Bible. Does the silence of the Scriptures imply prohibition or does it mean that the Christian is granted freedom in certain areas of church matters? This question was the fire; the society and the instrument served as the fuel.

Interestingly, the instrument made its debut in a Disciple worship service prior to the Civil War. The Disciples had already been exchanging punches over the ACMS for a little over seven years. Because of this, there was little notice about this unprecedented action, and it was several years before serious debate encompassed the brethren. For instance, David Lipscomb made no comment on the instrument until 1873.

Historians debate the exact date when instrumental music became a major issue in the Movement. Some suggest as early as 1851, while others argue that division over using an instrument in worship did not occur until the late 1880s. However, most agree that the debate broke out among adherents of the Movement in Kentucky.[1]

A logical starting point for the instrumental music controversy is 1864. In this year, the *Millennial Harbinger* contained several articles written by W.K. Pendleton and J.W. McGarvey on the issue. Also, during this year, Moses Lard (a former student of Campbell's at Bethany College) jumped into the fray by addressing the question in his publication, *Lard's Quarterly*. Clearly, this was the time the instrumental music question was taking root in the Movement.

The fight over the use of instrumental music in worship was not a new battle for the Disciples. It was a familiar one wearing different clothes. Back in 1805, historian Errett Gates pointed this out when he wrote, "The organ controversy was the missionary controversy in a new form, for both grew out of the opposition to human innovations in the work and worship of the church."[2]

Yet, the matter of worship is both a deeply personal matter and a matter of conscience. Therefore, arguments over matters of worship were fiercely fought.

The circumstances surrounding the introduction of the instrument at the congregation in Midway, Kentucky, by its

L. L. Pinkerton

minister, L.L. Pinkerton, were somewhat humorous. Pinkerton had introduced a melodeon, because of the horrible singing of the congregants. Evidently, from his comments, he had reached his "breaking point" in regard to the poor singing. The melodeon was originally used in Saturday night singing practice and in giving the correct pitch to begin each hymn on Sunday. However, it moved from practice to the Sunday worship, and the congregants felt that the instrument improved the singing.[3]

Yet, Pinkerton's action was not without opposition among the members at Midway. One of the elders attempted to dispose of the melodeon only to have his efforts thwarted when another melodeon was brought into the building to restore the one that was removed by his slave.

This new development began to attract the attention of Disciples leaders. With the slow decline of the *Millennial Harbinger,* due to the deteriorating health of Alexander Campbell, the *American Christian Review* began to ascend as the most popular journal among the Disciples. The *Review's* editor, Benjamin Franklin, decided to address the matter of instrumental music in worship.

There had already been limited discussion prior to Franklin's participation. Campbell had briefly discussed the issue in the pages of the *Harbinger.* While not harshly denouncing the use of the instrument in worship, Campbell, nevertheless, did not see the value of such use. He wrote,

> So to those who have no real devotion or spirituality in them, and whose animal nature flags under the oppression of church service, I think … that instrumental music would be not only a desideratum, but an essential prerequisite to fire up their souls to even animal devotion. But, I presume, to all spiritually-minded Christians, such aids would be as a cow bell in a concert.[4]

Franklin was even more direct in his comments. He wrote, "There is not a living church any place, in the spirit of Christ, making zealous and godly efforts to convert and save the world, with instrumental music in it."[5]

No more significant, brotherhood-wide discussion took place concerning the use of the instrument until 1864. The flame was rekindled by a letter and subsequent response by W.K. Pendleton in the *Harbinger*. The letter simply asked if the use of the instrument in worship was scriptural. The author of the letter, a person who identified himself as "Ancient Order," was concerned about the effect that an organ in worship had on the congregants. He argued that less people sang when an organ was used. Yet, instrumental music was not his only concern. He was also troubled by another innovation creeping into churches in the Movement: the song book, which he also felt was wrong.

Pendleton replied by giving a brief history of the instrument's rise in religion. He addressed the writer's concern that the use of an organ adversely affects congregational singing. He argued that nothing should be introduced that would harm this "privilege," and that he was opposed to anything which would interfere with congregational singing. However, Pendleton's response did not settle the issue for him or the rest of the Disciples. He wrote,

> But this does not settle the question after all—for there are many things established and right, in the practical affairs of the church in this 19th century, that were not introduced in the days, nor by the authority of the apostles—questions of mere expediency, that involve neither moral nor spiritual principle or teaching.[6]

The same year, J.W. McGarvey made public his position on the question of instrumental music. In an article for the *Harbinger* he wrote that one could argue for the use of the instrument based upon the silence of the scriptures, but he reasoned that this argument was inconclusive in light of the references to worship contained in the Old and New Testaments, as well as early church historical records. McGarvey also addressed the mention in the Bible of angels playing various instruments. Simply put, McGarvey stated that what may be permitted for angels, may not be permitted for people.

Calling readers to remember the beginning of the Movement, McGarvey wrote, "In the earlier years of the present Reformation, there was entire unanimity in the rejection of instrumental music from our public worship. It was declared unscriptural, inharmonious with the Christian institution, and a source of corruption.[7]

McGarvey realized that some would see his argument as inconsistent since he supported the ACMS, but opposed instrumental music. McGarvey argued that whether silence is permissive or prohibitive depends on the circumstances surrounding each individual case.

In his conclusion, McGarvey urged the brethren to study this matter and review his argument, which he believed was valid and the final word that needed to be spoken on the question. Needless to say, there were some Disciples who did not agree with McGarvey's conclusions.

In addition to the question of scriptural authority for the use of the instrument in worship, a quote from Barton Stone about the question of societies addressed what some Disciples may have been feeling about the instrument. Stone replied to an article written by Walter Scott in the *Christian Messenger* about church cooperation. He agreed with Scott's affirmation of such activity, but also added that the reason some people in the Movement opposed this type of endeavor was because it was too similar to what the Baptists were doing. This same attitude characterized some conservative Disciples who witnessed the instrument being introduced into various denominations and wished for the Movement to not pattern work or worship after the denominations.

The peaceful and cordial discussions were forever interrupted by the ascent of one of the most controversial Disciple leaders: Moses Lard. Lard secured his place in Disciples' history forever by being the first person to call for a break in fellowship over the instrumental music issue. For Lard, this matter was non-negotiable and contrary to the example of the early church.

Recognizing the autonomy of the congregations in the Movement, Lard knew that a brotherhood-wide resolution (though attempted on various matters by the ACMS) could not be imposed on the Disciples. In lieu of this, he outlined three actions that could effectively deal with this growing problem:

1. no preacher should enter a church building where an organ was in place;

2. no Disciple should unite with a pro-organ church; and

3. Disciples in individual congregations should oppose any attempts at the introduction of an instrument in "gentle, kind and decided terms." However, if opposition failed, then they should leave that congregation and begin another one.[8]

Despite the sweltering current of differing opinions on the instrument, the issue did not officially polarize the Disciples until after the Civil War, and unfortunately, after the death of Alexander Campbell. Then the issues of sectionalism combined with instrumental music to form a lethal merger that would prompt, together with the missionary society debate, formal division among the Disciples.

The congregation in Midway, Kentucky, secured its place in history as the first church in the Movement, on record, to introduce an instrument in worship. However, it was the intro-duction of an organ at a Disciple congregation in St. Louis in 1867 that brought the issue to the forefront. Surprisingly, the furor was not over the sole purpose of an organ, but over the purchase of a church building from an Episcopalian group, which included the organ in the building.

To purchase a building and have the organ part of the purchase, should have sent warning flags to those involved in the transaction. Whether this was the case or not, is not known. What is known is that almost immediately, the members discussed what should be done with the organ. The only elder at the church thought the organ should be used. A congregational vote took place in 1869, and the majority voted to use the instrument. Yet, the use of the organ was delayed until after 1870, when the pro-organ majority no longer conceded to those opposed to the instrument.[9]

St. Louis was not the only place where the instrument issue seized the attention of individual churches. In 1868, Benjamin

Franklin preached at the congregation in Akron, Ohio, and to his surprise, an organ was used during the worship. In the past when Franklin had visited, the congregation did not use the organ out of deference to Franklin and his opposition to such action, and, through this experience Franklin concluded that the majority of the congregation did not agree with using the instrument. This experience seemed to embolden Franklin's crusade against the use of instruments in worship. He later wrote, "If brethren will introduce the instrument into the worship, they shall themselves be held responsible . . . We know positively that it is safe to keep it out.[10]

During this time, Disciple churches in Chicago, Memphis and Cincinnati all brought in instruments. This was an issue that was not going to simply vanish and it had already become an issue that challenged the Movement's call to "union in truth."

It was in 1870 that Isaac Errett, editor of the *Christian Standard*, entered the discussion. Originally, Errett opposed using the instrument, but he encouraged a commitment to unity between differing brethren. Errett saw the issue as falling under the category of opinion. He understood the expediency argument but believed the instrument as unnecessary. His advice was to not use the instrument:

> We may as well state now, that we intend to counsel against the use of instrumental music in our churches. Our object is to persuade brethren who favor such to hold their preferences in abeyance for the sake of harmony for as the love of harmony is that which leads them to desire the employment of the organ, we wish them to see that the deeper and more precious harmony of soul must not be sacrificed."[11]

Then Errett stated a position he later clung to through the controversial dialogue concerning the instrument: "It is, we admit an important difference and needs to be adjusted; but being a difference of opinion, no man has a right to make it, on either side, a test of fellowship or an occasion of stumbling."[12]

While Errett sought to walk the safe path to help preserve the unity of the Disciples, others did not see Errett's position as safe or beneficial to the Movement. For some Disciples, the use of an instrument was not a matter of opinion, but a matter of faith. Upon this premise the debate would continue to rage. The problem for the Disciples was in distinguishing issues as matter of faith or matters of opinion. Errett believed the use of the instrument was not a matter of faith, and, therefore, a non-essential. Franklin thought otherwise and he clearly communicated his opposition. In his mind, those who "forced" instrumental music into worship at congregations were causing division.

> If you press the instrument into the worship, we care not whether you call it an element in the worship or an aid, and drive them away, because they cannot conscientiously worship with the instrument, you cause division – you are the aggressor—the innovator—you do this, too, for the accompaniment of corruption and apostasy, admitting at the same time that you have no conscience in the matter.

The facet of the debate that raged the fiercest at this time was the question of expediency. In 1868-69, Robert Richardson, Alexander Campbell's friend and biographer, and H.T. Anderson discussed this matter at length. Anderson believed that without a specific prohibition against the use of the instrument, one cannot say that its use constitutes a sin. Richardson disagreed, citing that expediency falls within the scope of the law. Therefore, the law comes first, then expediency. He wrote, "If it were anywhere said in the New Testament that Christians should use the instruments, then it would become a question of expediency what kind of instruments were to be used . . . and what circumstances should regulate their performance."[14]

Observing the debate from afar was a silent David Lipscomb. He had not publicly commented on the issue to date, but he was preparing to let the voice of the South be made known.

During the early years that Disciple leaders were taking verbal shots at one another over the use of the instrument, Lipscomb was busy in helping the South recover from the devastation caused by the Civil War. He had already taken a firm stand against the missionary society and seemed to have no interest in engaging the instrumental music debate. The South was recovering and from an economic standpoint, congregations could not afford to purchase organs or other instruments, so the question was a moot one.

However, Lipscomb's mentor, Tolbert Fanning, addressed the instrumental music question in an article in the 1856 issue of the *Gospel Advocate*. Included in this article was Fanning's famous declaration that instrumental music was a "mockery of all that is sacred." Fanning wrote, "It is scarcely necessary for us to say to our readers, that we regard the organ and violin worship, and even the fashionable choir singing of our country as a mockery of all that is sacred."[15]

When Lipscomb finally decided to comment on the controversy through the pages of the *Advocate*, his argument was more in agreement with what Richardson had earlier argued, than with the position Errett had taken. In Lipscomb's mind, the expediency argument set a dangerous precedent, for if one justifies a position based on expediency, then one sets a precedent that will prove hard to rebut when others seek to do the same with other beliefs. He wrote, "Again, if we open the door to expediency, where shall we close it? Why stop at the organ?"[16] Lipscomb also asserted that the argument which cites the use of the instrument in Old Testament times is invalid, because the Christian's primary instructions are received by Jesus Christ.

> Whatever Jesus found in Judaism that he approved, he retained in the Christian worship. Whatever he disapproved, he left out. He found the organ in use among the Jews. He left it out, failed to adopt it in the Christian worship. When Christ dropped it out, who dare place it in?[17]

The answer to the instrumental music question was a simple one to Lipscomb. His argument that abstaining from the use of the instrument is the safest way to worship was extremely similar to one of Franklin's earlier reasons. Lipscomb summed up this philosophy by writing, "Others accept the New Testament as their rule of faith, but do not make it the limit to their faith. . . . We seek for things authorized, they for things not prohibited. Our rule is safe—theirs is loose and latitudinarian."[18]

Lipscomb's argument was not merely based on what was safe. Lipscomb firmly believed that Jesus had rejected the instrument. This was his primary argument. In fact, he did not accept the argument of some that the use of the instrument should be avoided to keep from harming the consciences of other brethren. He believed this argument did not work, because Jesus had not rejected meat, whereas, in Lipscomb's mind, he had rejected the use of the instrument in worship.[19]

The missionary society and instrumental music in worship are commonly seen as the two primary issues that divided the Disciples, but these issues merely represented a much larger problem. These issues did not divide the Movement. These issues were symptoms of a much deeper question: how should a person interpret the Bible? Lipscomb believed that where the Bible remained silent, so should the Christian. Others who agreed with Lipscomb based such reasoning on sections of Thomas Campbell's *Declaration and Address*:

> If any circumstantials indispensably necessary to the observance of Divine ordinances be not found upon the page of express revelation, such, and such only, as are absolutely necessary for this purpose should be adopted under the title of human expedients.[20]

He argued that neither the society nor the instrument in worship were necessary for the church to function.

Compared with the number of articles written in opposition to the missionary society, Lipscomb wrote little about the use of the instrument. One reason for this is that he adamantly believed the argument used to justify the Society was the same argument used to justify the use of the instrumental music in worship. Only by closely following the Bible could the church maintain a course acceptable to God. Some called Lipscomb legalistic and ultra-conservative. Lipscomb was only deserving of the latter title.

In 1889, the voice of the true legalist roared.

"Nothing in life has given me more pain in heart than the separation from those I have heretofore worked with and loved."

— *David Lipscomb, 1899*

Division Made Official

The Churches of Christ Withdraw

*T*wo distinct groups within the Restoration Movement became apparent in the decades following the Civil War. Yet, no formal division was called by any of the leaders within the Movement. Ideologically, men like David Lipscomb and Isaac Errett symbolized the issues at hand that represented the two groups among the Disciples.

Lipscomb represented a conservative interpretation of Thomas Campbell's dictum: "Where the Scriptures speak, we speak; where the Scriptures are silent, we are silent." To Lipscomb this meant that if the Bible did not specifically authorize an action, then such action was prohibited. On the other hand, Errett represented the view which interpreted the silence of the Scriptures as freedom to act within general scriptural guidelines. The matter of interpretation was at the core of the rising wave of dissension among the Disciples.

While there are a number of matters that led to the impending division in 1906, the impact of the Civil War on the Movement cannot be overstated. The Civil War issues of slavery and pacifism increased the magnitude of the dispute and also brought matters to a head quicker than most likely would have happened. No single leader was as deeply impacted by the Civil War as Lipscomb, and no single Southern leader was destined to leave as significant a mark as the influential editor. The tremendous effect of the war, coupled with the debates over the missionary society (in particular, the loyalty resolutions) and instrumental music, gave rise to what soon became irreconcilable differences among the brethren.

Daniel Sommer

The fragile unity of the Disciples, however, was tested in a new way by a brazen Indiana preacher named Daniel Sommer.

Born during the infancy of the missionary society controversy, preceding the instrumental music question and the bitter Civil War, Sommer became one of the most interesting and difficult to understand leaders in the Restoration Movement. His chief enemy was personified in the innovations being introduced into churches in the Movement. His primary weapon was a biting sarcastic tone and an uncompromising attitude. His enduring legacy was an "Address and Declaration."

Sommer followed in the footsteps of his mentor, Benjamin Franklin. Yet, Sommer, unlike Franklin, would pursue a course that would split many of the Indiana Disciples from the rest of the Movement.

The place was Sand Creek, Illinois, and Sommer made a declaration against those Disciples who he thought were abandoning the heart of the American Restoration Movement through the acceptance of what Sommer termed "innovations." The purpose of Sand Creek was to draw a line of division. To this extent, it succeeded.

At least one historian equates Sommer and David Lipscomb, calling the two men the "two fathers" of the Churches of Christ.[1] Such an assertion is a stretch to make. Lipscomb and Sommer were two extremely different individuals. Sommer, ever the legalist, sought division. The influence of Alexander Campbell on this Indiana preacher was minimal. Lipscomb, on the other hand, did not seek division, although he recognized shortly after the turn of the century that division seemed to be inevitable. For Lipscomb, there was no joy in a division among the Disciples. Where Sommer found cause to rejoice, Lipscomb found cause to mourn.

"The Sand Creek Declaration and Address" took place in

1889 before an estimated crowd of 6,000 Disciples. Read by Peter P. Warren, one of the elders at Sand Creek, the document was nothing less than a formal call for division among the Disciples. This was the moment to which Sommer believed he had been called. His fight was against erroneous Disciples who were brethren in Christ. Such a focus made for an interesting ministry. Sommer himself made such an observation when he wrote, "Finally, I should mention that the work of saving a residue of the disciples of Christ imposed on me nearly all the chief controversies of my life over three-score years."[2]

Sommer's emphasis on the simplicity of the Bible led him to reach conclusions that Alexander Campbell, J.W. McGarvey, Isaac Errett, and David Lipscomb did not reach. However, what happened at Sand Creek was not a total surprise. Sommer had primed his readers for the event in the pages of his journal, the *Octographic Review*. Shortly after the mass meeting in Illinois, Sommer wrote an article entitled, "A Grand Occasion." This article relayed some of the events of this mass meeting between churches in Illinois. One of the matters of discussion, according to Sommer, was what to do with the brethren in the Movement who were seeking to "modernize" the church. Such a question indicated that a public division was in the works. Sommer responded by writing about the events at Sand Creek and admonished his readers to bring back the "modernizers" to a proper understanding of God's Church.[3]

The following month, Sommer published the speech he gave on August 17, 1889, at Sand Creek entitled, "An Address." This important speech given by Sommer was followed by the reading of an equally important document called "The Address and Declaration," read by Peter Warren. Both documents called for division. As any able politician would do before invoking the storms of controversy, Sommer established the common ground he and his hearers shared. He began his speech in sermon-fashion, emphasizing the power of faith. He did this in context with knowing the "divine will" of God. Sommer made his point by writing, "In other words, whatever the word of God declares with approbation we can believe has been or now is the will of God; but whatever the word of God does not thus declare we not only DO NOT but we CANNOT believe has ever been the will of God."[4]

Sommer, in ascribing to the hermeneutical view that states anything not specifically commanded by the Bible is prohibited, was in accordance with Lipscomb's view about the silence of the Scriptures. However, as was seen later in his speech, Sommer was more willing to make a clean break with those Disciples with whom he disagreed. Sommer's action is not what was amazing about this situation; what was amazing is that an estimated 6,000 people voiced their approval of such action. Clearly, Sand Creek was not a passing tremor within the Movement.

Sommer's speech concluded with a list of seven charges against those whom he termed "innovators." Before reaching the list of charges, though, Sommer expressed his strong belief that these "innovators" were abandoning the very principles that made the Disciples unique among religious groups.

> Returning now to our original theme, I call heaven and earth, men and angels to witness that the discrimination between testimony and inference, and between faith and opinion—this discrimination which made disciples a great and a mighty and a separate people—this discrimination which has given us our peculiar strength and power as teachers of this religious and irreligious world—I say that I call heaven and earth, angels and men to witness that THIS DISCRIMINATION HAS BY INNOVATORS AMONG DISCIPLES BEEN ABANDONED.[5]

The charges which followed were based on the intangible, as well as tangible actions of those Sommer called the "modern school brethren." Sommer charged that the insistence of these brethren to bring innovations into the church had caused them to be "responsible for every restless, sleepless night and unhappy day." Simply put, Sommer blamed the "innovators" for every negative situation among the Disciples. The only peace that could come among the Disciples would be if the "innovators" mended their ways. If this did not happen, Sommer was prepared to lead a group of Disciples into a new denomination.

The crowd continued to hear the call for division when Warren read the "Address and Declaration" following Sommer's speech. He began in the same way Sommer did, by building an argument for the silence of the Scriptures. His list of charges was against church festivals, organized missionary work, and the located preacher.[6]

The elders from the five congregations represented at Sand Creek felt these matters were so severe that the only course of action left for them to take was to breach fellowship with those who advocated such matters. Thus the influence of Sommer was tremendous as is seen in the concluding statement of the document read by Warren:

> And now, in closing up this address and declaration, we state that we are impelled from a sense of duty to say, that all such as are guilty of teaching, or allowing and practicing the many innovations to which we have referred, that after being admonished and having had sufficient time for reflection, if they do not turn away from such abominations, that we can not and will not regard them as brethren.[7]

The events at Sand Creek brought a swift response from the Christian Standard. An unidentified author, whose disgust was evident through his sarcastic writing made these comments, "Sand Creek is immortal. Sand Creek has taken lessons of the Pope who issued his bull against the comet. Sand Creek will live forever!"[8]

Lipscomb did not respond through the pages of the Gospel Advocate until three years later. While agreeing with Sommer's premises, Lipscomb still saw the mass meeting and its subsequent actions as without scriptural authority. In fact, he pointed out that the leaders at Sand Creek had committed actions which they were railing against others for committing. "This looks very much like a convention unknown to the New Testament exercising judicial and executive functions to oppose error and maintain truth, and it looks very much like doing the thing they condemn."[9]

Lipscomb, even though agreeing with the positions of the leaders at Sand Creek, nevertheless saw the inconsistency of what had happened at Sand Creek with what these Disciples were trying to accomplish. Lipscomb wrote, "It has been the besetting sin of Christians, when they start out to oppose a wrong, to commit another wrong to oppose this."[10]

During this time Lipscomb struggled with what he saw as a growing division within the Movement. He recognized it and it pained him greatly, yet he also believed there were some in the Movement who were leaving behind some of the Movement's early tenets.

This division was not a desire of Lipscomb, but a recognition of a harsh reality. Lipscomb recognized the seriousness of the stand he took and its subsequent ramifications, but he could not recant. Union with God, in Lipscomb's mind, was the one true union that mattered.

While deeply committed to Campbell's efforts at unity, Lipscomb also could not disavow his belief concerning the silence of the Scriptures. He believed that the churches of Christ had "started on the road to apostasy."[11] The Civil War's impact on the division was seen in the methods used to argue the issues surrounding the war. When Lipscomb argued the case for the Christian's non-participation in government, he did so from the silence of the Scriptures. When arguments were made for or against slavery, they were based on one's interpretation of the Bible. The Civil War was the practice field where the methodology of the arguments which would later formally divide the Movement developed.

The official declaration that occurred in 1906 was a decision that tore at the heart of Lipscomb. At least one historian surmises that Lipscomb did not view division as inevitable until 1899.[12]

He had developed much of his mindset from Fanning, who was greatly influenced by Alexander Campbell. It was not Lipscomb's intention to be part of a division among the Disciples. The estrangement between himself and the supporters of the American Christian Missionary Society was particularly difficult for Lipscomb. However, he was still invited to join in the celebration of the fiftieth anniversary of the Society in 1899. Lipscomb, though, declined the invitation. His decision did not come easy and in making it, Lipscomb suffered much heartache. He candidly expressed his feelings when he wrote,

> Nothing in life has given me more pain in heart than the separation from those I have heretofore worked with and loved. The majority seem to be going away and leaving those who stand firm for the old ways. I love to be with the majority, and would certainly go with them, if I were not afraid of offending God in so doing.[13]

Lipscomb found himself backed into a corner. He received criticism both from the more conservative elements and the more progressive elements of the Movement. He attempted to stand in the gap as the voice of a moderate, only to endure the criticism that the Civil War had spawned. He urged the conservatives in the Movement to be careful of their rhetoric and of their dialogue with those with whom they were in disagreement:

> The weakness of those who claim to be loyal to God is not the opposition of the 'progressives,' as they are called, but it is the fault-finding, distrust, and strife among themselves over untaught questions, over questions that constitute no part of the faith of God. We lose sight of our own growth in grace and the salvation of souls in contentions about questions in which there is no profit.[14]

Not able to ever fully reconcile with Errett or those of like mindset, Lipscomb grew skeptical of maintaining unity in the Movement. The failed attempts at bridging the gap between him and J.W. McGarvey were also disheartening. When Lipscomb responded to the bureau of the U.S. Census in 1906, stating that the churches of Christ were a separate group from the rest of the American Restoration Movement, he did so with a great burden on his heart. He had remained optimistic about preserving the fragile unity of the Movement, but Lipscomb came to believe that the acceptance of the ACMS had paved the way for the entrance of a host of maladies into the Movement.

Yet, the Civil War still loomed large over the division of the

Disciples. The widening ideological gap between North and South was seen in a variety of social and sectional issues. The North, which had come through the war in relatively good condition, began its ascent up the ladder of progress. This progress not only centered in industry and technology, but also spilled over into the realm of religion. Northern Disciples were desirous of improvements and progress in their methods. The Southern Disciples, undergoing the massive reconstruction efforts, were nowhere near the abilities of Northern industry. Southern Disciples attempted to hold onto a simple religious faith, showcased in a strict interpretation of the Bible.

No one can dispute that there were a variety of issues concerning the splintering of the Disciples. These issues are significant because the philosophical background to the arguments over issues like pacifism and slavery was the same philosophical background behind the arguments about missionary societies and instrumental music in worship. Interestingly, the developing philosophies, formed in drastically different social settings, were seen in Southerners embracing a literal interpretation of the Bible while certain segments in the North progressed in the other direction.

It is unlikely that the Disciples would have been spared division if the Civil War had never taken place. The division seemed inevitable. What the Civil War did was make it a reality sooner than expected. The story of the second generation of American Restoration Movement leaders, in particular, Lipscomb, is a story of brotherhood fellowship, the role that matters of faith play in that fellowship, and the pain that comes when brethren disagree over what they believe are matters of faith. Lipscomb was a flawed leader, as were all the leaders among the Disciples. One can either appreciate the good accomplished by Lipscomb, fully understanding the mistakes he made, or one can dismiss him as a divisive leader.

The latter option will lead to more schisms within the American Restoration Movement and make the plea of "union in truth" that much harder for anyone to hear.

Timeline

1842 . . . . .First cooperation meeting in Tennessee

1844 . . . . .Barton W. Stone dies

1845 . . . . .D.S. Burnet begins the American Christian Bible
Society

1849 . . . . .Birth of American Christian Missionary Society

1850 . . . . .Connellsville (PA) church opposed ACMS

1852 . . . . .Jesse Ferguson controversy

1854 . . . . .Thomas Campbell dies

1855 . . . .*Gospel Advocate* begins

1857 . . . . .Fanning-Richardson controversy

1859 . . . . .Instrument introduced in Midway, Kentucky

1861 . . . . .Civil War begins and Walter Scott dies

1863 . . . . .ACMS Loyalty Resolutions

1866 . . . . .Alexander Campbell dies; *Christian Standard*
begins

1869 . . . . .Feud between Lipscomb and McGarvey

1874 . . . . .Tolbert Fanning dies

1878 . . . . .Benjamin Franklin dies

1880 . . . . .Lipscomb and Isaac Errett conflict

1888 . . . . .Isaac Errett dies

1889 . . . . .Daniel Sommer and Sand Creek

1906 . . . . .Division among Disciples officially recognized

Leaders of the American Restoration Movement

Thomas Campbell
(1763-1854)

*F*ather of Alexander and author of the most important document for adherents of the American Restoration Movement, next to the Bible: *The Declaration and Address.* Campbell had grown tired of religious wrangling, the making of creeds and confessions of faith as tests of communion. His grievances against followers of Christ were seen in his fight against sectarianism and his desire for the unity of all who call themselves Christian.

His *Declaration and Address* contained thirteen propositions, the most famous of which was the first one which stated, "The Church of Christ upon earth is essentially, intentionally, and constitutionally one; consisting of all those in every place that profess their faith in Christ and obedience to him in all things according to the Scriptures, and that manifest the same by their tempers and conduct, and of none else; as none else can be truly and properly called Christians."

Though not as much in the forefront as his son, Alexander, the elder Campbell still had a tremendous influence on the American Restoration Movement as it continued to grow.

Alexander Campbell
(1788-1866)

Son of Thomas and the most recognizable face among the leaders of the American Restoration Movement. Campbell embarked on a life-long quest to unite followers of Christ by one standard, the Bible. Even though those who ascribe to Campbell's ideas refer to their movement as the American Restoration Movement, Campbell never used such a term. He preferred to call the young movement a reformatory one. He was not in the business of creating a new denomination. Rather, he sought to unite followers of Christ.

Campbell founded Bethany College (founded in 1841 and still in existence) and edited two influential journals in the Movement: the *Christian Baptist* (*begun in 1823*) and the *Millennial Harbinger* (*begun in 1830*).

Campbell insisted on "free discussion." He urged Disciples to not draw lines of fellowship unless a clear scriptural command could be found. On divisive matters such as slavery and the American Christian Missionary Society, Campbell pleaded for toleration, stating that these issues should never become tests of fellowship.

Though his influence declined in later years, and some people accused others of using Campbell's name to their advantage, his mere presence continued to have a dramatic impact on the Disciples.

Among the first-generation of leadership with the American Restoration Movement, Campbell was the only leader to live through the Civil War.

Barton Warren Stone
(1772-1844)

*B*arton Stone filled a crucial role with the American Restoration Movement. He left a legacy of Christian unity, commitment to scriptural authority, and forbearance with others of differing opinions.

He was present at the great Cane Ridge Revival in 1801 and was part of a group of Presbyterian ministers who withdrew from the Synod of Kentucky. They, in turn, formed the Springfield Presbytery, which consisted of fifteen churches – seven in Ohio and eight in Kentucky. But the Presbytery was short-lived. In fact, the men dissolved the Presbytery on June 28, 1804. They did so with an incredibly significant document known as the "Last Will and Testament of the Springfield Presbytery." The desired to be known simply as Christians and to promote the union of all followers of Christ.

Stone edited the *Christian Messenger* (begun in 1826) and continued, throughout the remainder of his life, to advocate and promote the unity of Christians. He fought for this unity within the boundaries of Scripture. He firmly believed that Christians could be guided solely by Scripture and still be united.

Walter Scott
(1796-1861)

*R*eferred to as the "evangelist" of the American Restoration Movement, Scott's influence is still felt throughout churches connected with the Movement. His five-finger plan of salvation still echoes through halls of church buildings and in Bible studies.

Significantly influenced by John Locke and Sir Francis Bacon, Scott placed a great emphasis on the use of reason in leading people to Christ. He preached the "Gospel Restored" and accentuated baptism for the remission of sins, on which he wrote a lengthy discourse entitled, *The Gospel Restored. A Discourse of the True Gospel of Jesus Christ, in Which the Facts, Principles, Duties, and Priviliges [sic] of Christianity are Arranged, Defined, and Discussed, and the Gospel in its Various Parts Shewn to be Adapted to the Nature and Necessities of Man in His Present Condition.*

His ministry revolved around the great truth that Jesus is the Messiah, the Son of God. This claim, Scott believed, was a key to the unity of all followers of Christ.

He died at the beginning of the Civil War, fearful that the Movement's great dreams were going to explode as the cannonballs hit Fort Sumter.

Tolbert Fanning
(1810-1874)

*I*nfluenced by Alexander Campbell, Fanning exerted a tremendous influence on Disciples in the South, particularly in Tennessee. He founded Franklin College in 1845, *The Christian Review* in 1844, and the *Gospel Advocate* in 1855, which became the most influential journal among Southern Disciples.

Fanning, though one of the original twenty-nine vice presidents of the American Christian Missionary Society, spent considerable time decrying the national organization. He was a promoter of intrastate cooperation between churches, but became vigorously opposed to the ACMS, especially after the "loyalty resolutions" of 1861 and 1863.

As David Lipscomb's mentor, Fanning helped shape the views of Lipscomb, and thus maintained a large presence among the Disciples even after his death in 1874. In addition to teaching against the ACMS, Fanning also fought against the introduction of instruments in worship.

David Lipscomb
(1831-1917)

Mentored by Tolbert Fanning and indirectly influenced by Alexander Campbell, Lipscomb came to leadership within the Movement during a time of controversy and religious wrangling. He believed in the unity of all followers of Christ, but was unable to reconcile this quest for unity with what he felt were the introduction of practices contrary to the teachings of Scripture.

He edited the *Gospel Advocate*, which was founded by his older brother William Lipscomb and Fanning, for forty-six years. Throughout the pages of the *Advocate*, Lipscomb sought to provide guidance for Disciples in the South.

Lipscomb was one of the founders of Nashville Bible School in 1891, which is now David Lipscomb University. His influence continues among churches of Christ, particularly churches of Christ in the South. Heart-broken at the division within the American Restoration Movement, Lipscomb carried on his ministry of calling people back to the Scriptures as their only guide for faith and practice.

Isaac Errett
(1820-1888)

One of the most influential leaders among the Northern Disciples, Errett sought to preserve the fragile unity of the Disciples, but found himself enveloped in controversy for his part in the "loyalty resolutions" passed by the American Christian Missionary Society in 1861 and 1863.

Errett promoted the ACMS and also argued against those in the Movement who denounced instrumental music as a sin. For Errett, the use of the instrument in worship was a matter of opinion, and, one could argue, a matter of expediency.

He edited the *Christian Standard* (founded in 1866), which became the most significant journal for Northern Disciples.

Benjamin Franklin
(1812-1878)

One of the important leaders among the Northern Disciples, and a leader who seemed to appeal to both Northern and Southern Disciples, Franklin was thrust into the midst of controversy over issues like the American Christian Missionary Society and instrumental music in worship.

Founder and editor of the *American Christian Review* (founded in 1856), Franklin waged war against what he viewed as innovations in the Movement. With the declining health of Alexander Campbell, the Review became, for a few years, the most influential journal among the Disciples.

Though initially supporting the ACMS, Franklin switched positions and spent years speaking against national organizations like the ACMS.

David Staats Burnet
(1808-1867)

Burnet dreamed of world-wide evangelism and sought to bring this dream into reality by creating organizations like the American Christian Bible Society and the American Christian Missionary Society. However, his dreams quickly denigrated into controversy as Disciples took sides on such issues.

Burnet even quarreled with Alexander Campbell over the creation of national societies. Eventually, though Campbell bought into the idea and became the first president, in abstentia, of the ACMS.

Though often overlooked, Burnet played an important role as the American Restoration Movement sought to organize for the purpose of world-wide evangelism.

J. W. McGarvey
(1829-1911)

McGarvey, who served as professor of sacred theology at the College of the Bible in Lexington, Kentucky, became the voice of scholarship among second-generation leadership in the Movement. McGarvey fought against "higher criticism" and maintained a commitment to a conservation approach to biblical interpretation, which emphasized reason and logic.

He advocated the merits of the American Christian Missionary Society and fought vigorously against the introduction of instruments into worship assemblies. Though agreeing on many issues with David Lipscomb, the two men were unable to join on the common ground.

His writing, in particular his commentaries, still continues to influence adherents of the Movement today.

Daniel Sommer
(1850-1940)

Railing against what he thought were unscriptural innovations being introduced into churches throughout the Movement, Sommer became a central figure in the Movement's division.

In 1889, in front of a crowd estimated at 6,000 Disciples, Sommer advocated the separation from those who were erring in their religious practices.

Sommer, through the pages of his *Octographic Review*, called his readers to break fellowship and not regard as brethren those who used such innovations.

Notes

Chapter 1—Beginning

1. James B. North. *Union in Truth: An Interpretive History of the Restoration Movement* (Cincinnati: The Standard Publishing Company, 1994), 55.

2. Thomas H. Olbricht and Hans Rollman, *Thomas Campbell's Declaration and Address*, (Lanham, Maryland, 2000), 18.

3. Ibid.

Chapter 2—The State of the Movement

1. Tolbert Fanning, "The Crisis," *Christian Review*, Vol. 2, No. 10 (October 1845), 217-218.

2. Robert Richardson, "Faith versus Philosophy," *Millennial Harbinger* (1857), 267-268

3. Robert Hooper, *Crying in the Wilderness: A Biography of David Lipscomb* (Nashville, TN, 1979), 49.

4. Barton Warren Stone, *Christian Messenger* (1826), 15-16.

5. Alexander Campbell, *Christian Baptist* (March 7, 1825), 133.

Chapter 3—Slavery

1. Richard T. Hughes. *Reviving the Ancient Faith: The Story of Churches of Christ in America* (Grand Rapids: Michigan: William B. Eerdmans Publishing Company, 1996), 271.

2. Alexander Campbell, "The Crisis," *Millennial Harbinger* (1832), 87-88.

3. Ibid.

4. Robert Richardson, *Memoirs of Alexander Campbell*, Vol. 2 (Philadelphia: J.B. Lippincott & Co., 1870), 531.

5. Barton Stone, "An Humble Address to Christians, on the Colonization of Free People of Color," *Christian Messenger* (1828), 198.

6. James R. Wilburn, *The Hazard of the Die: Tolbert Fanning and the Restoration Movement* (Austin: Sweet Publishing, CO., 1969), 24.

7. Ibid.

8. Hooper, 19-20.

9. Ibid, 21.

10. Earl I. West. *The Life and Times of David Lipscomb* Reprint. (Germantown, Tennessee: Religious Book Service, 1987), 39.

11. Henry Webb, "Sectional Conflict and Schism Within the Disciples of Christ Following the Civil War," *Essays on New Testament Christianity* (The Standard Publishing Company, 1978), 118-119.

12. Benjamin Franklin, *American Christian Review* (March 15, 1859), 42.

13. Alexander Campbell, "Our Position to American Slavery—No. V," *Millennial Harbinger* (May 1845), 223.

14. J.S. Lamar. *Memoirs of Isaac Errett* (2 vols, Cincinnati: The Standard Publishing Co., 1893), I, 215.

Chapter 4—Brother against Brother

1. Alexander Campbell, "An Address on War," Printed in *Popular Lectures and Addresses*. (Nashville: Harbinger Book Club, n.d.), 342.

2. Ibid, 350.

3. Ibid, 352.

4. Ibid, 357.

5. West, 91.

6. Ibid, 92-93.

7. David Lipscomb. *Civil Government: Its Origin, Mission, and Destiny and the Christian's Relation to It* (Nashville: Gospel Advocate Company, 1957), 10-11.

8. Ibid, 58.

9. Ibid, 87.

10. "Circular from Preachers in Missouri," *Millennial Harbinger* (June 1861), 583-584.

11. Dwight E. Stevenson. *Walter Scott, Voice of the Golden Oracle: A Biography* Joplin, MO: College Press, 1946, 220.

12. Isaac Errett, "The Claims of Civil Government: A Sermon Delivered on the National Fast Day, April 30, 1863, in the Christian Church, Detroit, Michigan." (Detroit: O.S. Gulley's Steam Presses, 1863), 18 pages.

13. Ibid.

14. Hooper, 76.

15. Isaac Errett, "Religion and Politics," *Christian Standard* (October 20, 1866), 228.

16. Hooper, 84-85.

17. Moses E. Lard, "Should Christians go to War?" *Lard's Quarterly*, April 1866, 226.

18. Ibid.

19. Ibid, 227.

Chapter 5—Torn Asunder

1. D.S. Burnet, "Address: To the Churches of God in the United States, and to our fellow-citizens generally, in behalf of the American Christian Bible Society, organized in Cincinnati, January 27, 1845." *Millennial Harbinger*, 1845, 371.

2. Alexander Campbell, "Remarks," *Millennial Harbinger* (1845), 372-373.

3. Burnet, "American Christian Bible Society," *Millennial Harbinger* (1845), 453.

4. Ibid, 454.

5. Campbell, "Strictures on the Above," *Millennial Harbinger* (1845), 456.

6. Earl I. West. *The Search for the Ancient Order, Vol. 1, A History of the Restoration Movement 1849-1865* (Nashville: Gospel Advocate Company, 1964), 167.

7. Wilburn, 161.

8. "The Christian Missionary Society," *Millennial Harbinger*, 1850, 282-284.

9. West, 153.

Chapter 6—Sectionalism

1. James DeForest Murch, *Christians Only: A History of the Restoration Movement* (Cincinnati: The Standard Publishing Company, 1973), 154.

2. West, Vol. 1, 176.

3. J. S. Lamar, 270-271.

4. Murch, 154.

5. Tolbert Fanning, "Ministers of Peace in the World's Conflicts," *Gospel Advocate*, November 1861, 347-348.

6. Ibid.

7. David Lipscomb, "I Did Wrong," *Gospel Advocate*, March 13, 1866, 170-171.

8. Wilburn, 250.

9. David Edwin Harrell, *Quest for a Christian America: The Disciples of Christ and American Society to 1866* (Nashville: The Disciples of Christ Historical Society, 1966), 159.

10. Ibid, 163.

11. Ibid, 164.

12. Ibid, 161.

13. Ibid, 162.

14. William K. Pendleton, "American Christian Missionary Society," *Millennial Harbinger*, September 1864, 419.

Chapter 7—Brothers at Odds

1. Hooper, 95.
2. Ibid.
3. David Filbeck. *The First Fifty Years: A Brief History of the Direct-Support Missionary Movement* (Joplin, MO: College Press Publishing Company, 1980), 19.
4. Lamar, 300.
5. Filbeck, 30-31.
6. Ibid, 32-33.
7. Robert Milligan, "Missionary Societies," *Christian Standard*, November 10, 1866, 250.
8. Robert Richardson, "Missionary Work No. 2," *Christian Standard*, June 29, 1867, 201.
9. Tolbert Fanning, "The Church of Christ, No.1, *Gospel Advocate*, November, 1855, 134.
10. North, 243.
11. Hooper, 96.
12. Ibid, 284.
13. Ibid, 282.
14. David Lipscomb, *Gospel Advocate*, 1891, 792.
15. Hooper, 283.
16. Ibid, 284.
17. North, 264.
18. David Lipscomb, *Gospel Advocate*, 1889, 1153.
19. Filbeck, 37.
20. Hooper, 287.
21. *Gospel Advocate*, 1897, 578.
22. Leroy Garrett. T*he Stone-Campbell Movement: An Anecdotal History of Three Churches* (Joplin, Missouri: College Press Publishing Company, 1981), 609.

Chapter 8—The Effect of Silence in Worship

1. North, 221.

2. Errett Gates. *The Disciples of Christ* (New York: The Baker & Taylor Co., 1905), 250.

3. North, 222.

4. Alexander Campbell, "Instrumental Music," *Millennial Harbinger*, September 1851, 582.

5. Benjamin Franklin, "Instrumental Music in Churches," *American Christian Review*, January 31, 1860, 19.

6. W.K. Pendleton, "Pew-Renting and Organ Music," *Millennial Harbinger*, March 1864, 126-128.

7. Ibid. 126-128.

8. Moses E. Lard, "Instrumental Music in Churches and Dancing," *Lard's Quarterly*, March, 1864, 331.

9. West, Vol. 2, 81.

10. Benjamin Franklin, "Notes by the Way," *American Christian Review*, May 19, 1868, 156.

11. Isaac Errett, "Instrumental Music in Our Churches," *Christian Standard*, May 7, 1870, 148.

12. Ibid, 148.

13. Franklin, "Two Standards," *American Christian Review*, June 14, 1870, 188.

14. Robert Richardson, "Expediency," *Christian Standard*, 1868, 409.

15. Tolbert Fanning, "The Church of Christ, No. 9," *Gospel Advocate*, July 1856, 199.

16. David Lipscomb, "The Organ in Worship," *Gospel Advocate*

17. Ibid.

18. Ibid, 855.

19. Hooper, 170

20. Thomas Campbell, *The Declaration and Address*, 26.

Chapter 9—Division Made Official

1. Garret, 105.

2. William E. Wallace. *Daniel Sommer: A Biography* (n.p., 1969), 254.

3. Daniel Sommer. "A Grand Occasion," *Octographic Review*, August 29, 1889.

4. Ibid, "An Address," *Octographic Review*, September 5, 1889.

5. Ibid, 16.

6. "Address and Declaration," 19.

7. Ibid, 20.

8. "Sand Creek Chronicles," *Christian Standard*, September 28, 1889.

9. David Lipscomb, "Sand Creek Address and Declaration." *Gospel Advocate*, November 7, 1892, 725.

10. Ibid.

11. Hooper, 298.

12. Ibid.

13. David Lipscomb, *Gospel Advocate*, 1899, 104.

14. Ibid, 424.

Bibliography

Filbeck, David. *The First Fifty Years: A Brief History of the Direct-Support Missionary Movement.* Joplin: College Press Publishing Company, 1980.

Garrett, Leroy. *The Stone-Campbell Movement: An Anecdotal History of Three Churches.* Joplin: College Press Publishing Company, 1981.

Gates, Errett. *The Disciples of Christ.* New York: The Baker & Taylor Co., 1905.

Goodpasture, B. C. *Popular Lectures and Addresses by Alexander Campbell.* Nashville: Harbinger Book Club, n.d.

Harrell, David E. *Quest for a Christian America: The Disciples of Christ and American Society to 1866.* Nashville: The Disciples of Christ Historical Society, 1966.

Hooper, Robert. *Crying in the Wilderness: A Biography of David Lipscomb.* Nashville: David Lipscomb College, 1979.

Hughes, Richard T. *Reviving the Ancient Faith: The Story of Churches of Christ in America.* Grand Rapids: William B. Eerdmans Publishing Company, 1996.

Lamar, J.S. *Memoirs of Isaac Errett.* 2 vols. Cincinnati: The Standard Publishing Co., 1893.

Lipscomb, David. *Civil Government: Its Origin, Mission, and Destiny and the Christian's Relation to It.* Nashville: Gospel Advocate Company, 1957.

Murch, James DeForest. *Christians Only: A History of the Restoration Movement.* Cincinnati: The Standard Publishing Company, 1973.

North, James B. *Union in Truth: An Interpretive History of the Restoration Movement.* Cincinnati: The Standard Publishing Company, 1994.

Olbricht, Thomas H., and Rollman, Hans. *Thomas Campbell's Declaration and Address.* Lanham, Maryland: Scarecrow Press, 2000.

Richardson, Robert. *Memoirs of Alexander Campbell.* 2 vols. Philadelphia: J.B. Lippincott & Co., 1870.

Stevenson, Dwight E. *Walter Scott, Voice of the Golden Oracle: A Biography.* Joplin: College Press Publishing Company, 1946.

Wallace, William E. *Daniel Sommer: A Biography.* n.p., 1969.

West, Earl, I. *The Life and Times of David Lipscomb.* Reprint. Germantown: Religious Book Service, 1987.

_____. *The Search for the Ancient Order: A History of the Restoration Movement, 1849-1865.* 4 vols. Nashville: Gospel Advocate Company, 1964.

Wilburn, James R. *The Hazard of the Die: Tolbert Fanning and the Restoration Movement.* Austin: Sweet Publishing, Co., 1969.

Articles

Webb, Henry. "Sectional Conflict and Schism Within the Disciples of Christ Following the Civil War," *Essays on New Testament Christianity* (1978): 118-119.

Periodicals

American Christian Review.

Christian Baptist.

Christian Messenger.

Christian Review.

Christian Standard.

Gospel Advocate.

Lard's Quarterly.

Millennial Harbinger.

Octographic Review.